Writing and the Body

THE NORTHCLIFFE LECTURES
1981

Writing and the Body

GABRIEL JOSIPOVICI

PRINCETON UNIVERSITY PRESS
Princeton, New Jersey

Published by Princeton University Press,
41 William Street, Princeton, New Jersey

Copyright © 1982 by Gabriel Josipovici

ISBN 0-691-06550-0
LCC number 82-9042

Printed in Great Britain

To George Craig

'It seems so dreadful to stay a bachelor, to become an old man struggling to keep one's dignity while begging for an invitation whenever one wants to spend an evening in company, to lie ill gazing for weeks into an empty room from the corner where one's bed is, always having to say good night at the front door, never to run up a stairway beside one's wife, to have only side-doors in one's room leading into other people's living-rooms, having to carry one's supper home in one's hand, having to admire other people's children and not even being allowed to go on saying: "I have none myself", modelling oneself in appearance and behaviour on one or two bachelors remembered from one's youth.

That's how it will be, except that in reality both today and later, one will stand there with a palpable body and a real head, a real forehead, that is, for smiting on with one's hand.'

KAFKA

'What is yours to bestow is not yours to reserve.'

SHAKESPEARE

Contents

Preface

In the summer of 1979 I was invited to deliver the Lord Northcliffe Lectures at University College, London, for the 1980-81 session. What follows is substantially the lectures as I gave them, though the exigencies of time forced me to shorten one or two of them slightly when I delivered them.

The invitation was to give four lectures on 'whatever you happen to be working on'. I was embarrassed to admit that I was not 'working on' anything, and that all I could imagine myself at work on in a year's time would be a novel or play. Clearly I was not being invited to read from that kind of work in progress. At the same time, as far as I was concerned, the invitation had come at a most appropriate moment. I had just finished a novel on which I had been working with great intensity for fifteen months, and one's spirits are never so low as in the immediate aftermath of such an effort. One feels as if one has been talking for as long as one can remember into an unpeopled void, and whatever enthusiasm buoyed one up at the start of the enterprise has evaporated by the end; one is left only with the sense of waste, frustration and failure. To be asked at this juncture to talk to a group of interested people about a subject of my choice was an unexpected tonic. I immediately accepted.

But what subject should I choose? I had not realised till then how difficult this sort of assignment could be. To give a single lecture on a subject of one's choice is not too difficult; to give four lectures on a specific subject is also relatively easy. But to be asked to give four lectures on any subject one wants raises very real problems. For what *did* I want to talk about? What did I want to spend the next year thinking and reading about?

I realised early on that I was faced with at least one clear set of alternatives: I could either look at an apparently extremely limited subject in considerable detail in order to show that even this raised problems for reading and criticism which four lectures would be only just sufficient to bring out into the open (the relation of background to foreground in the first paragraph of *A la recherche*, and the nature of the gaps in Eliot's poetry were topics that came to mind); or I could tackle a subject so vast that though a book might seem pretentious and impossibly ambitious, four lectures could be seen as a personal and preliminary set of moves, designed more to raise questions than to provide answers. The special constraints of the lecture form — no more matter than can be comfortably delivered in one hour — ; but also its special privileges — direct contact with an audience, and thus the audience's constant awareness of the subjective and personal nature of the discourse — made the second option all the more attractive, and this is what I finally chose.

There was naturally a strong temptation to tinker with the lectures after they had been delivered, to try and fill out and develop some of the themes prior to publication. But to have succumbed to the temptation would have led the reader to ask, and rightly: Why have you stopped there? Why have you not rewritten the whole thing? Why have you not dealt with this aspect of the subject, or that? And then I would have been landed with just what I had wanted to avoid. I would have found myself in the position of trying to defend a thesis against all possible attack, instead of merely exploring certain issues which had seemed important to me. Since I believe no thesis is ever fully defensible, and since I am not sure if I even have a thesis (it feels more like a set of nagging worries), I have resisted the temptation and left the lectures as I wrote them to be delivered.

But to return to the question of the subject. A series of four lectures clearly requires a degree of commitment not demanded by one lecture. It cannot be built round a passing or peripheral interest; it must be concerned with something of absolutely central interest. As I thought about what I might like to speak about, I began to wonder if *any* subject would be able to claim my commitment in this way. Why spend a year on a reconsideration of the *nouveau roman*, on the strengths and weaknesses of recent critical theory, on the striking parallels between the *Commedia* and *A la recherche*? These were all important and fascinating subjects, subjects I had given some thought to and about which I felt I might have something of interest to say. They were *all* fascinating, *all* worth while. That was the problem. And by the same token none was so utterly absorbing that I felt I absolutely *had* to tackle it.

Was it simply a case of my inability to make up my mind? Was I being lazy, just wanting to defer any decision which would force me to get down to work? Or did the trouble perhaps lie with the subjects I was hesitating over? Was there not perhaps something I *really* wanted to write about, behind all of these, but which somehow I was not clear-headed enough to discern? Of course in such situations one can never be sure, but something told me I should trust my instinct, and my instinct told me it was not just a personal difficulty I was facing. And then it began to dawn on me that my subject might lie not on the other side of the confusion, of the thicket of conflicting desires in which I seemed to be caught, but in the nature of the confusion itself. My subject was not another topic, but the nature of choice itself, of the act of commitment to one subject rather than another.

As I began to understand what it was I might be after I also became aware of the fact that this rather precise question about the subject-matter of a series of lectures overlapped with something I had often been vaguely aware of but which I would never have previously thought of dignifying with the name of problem or topic. This was something which concerned the writing of fiction. While one is at work on an extended piece of fiction (and I imagine it is the same with painting and music) one has no desire to see anyone or to read anything. Everything seems to be an intrusion. It is not so much that one is afraid the book might be damaged by such contact — though that comes into it — as that nothing interests one except what one is working on. This total absorption is a blessing. But it is also a tyranny. As one nears the end of such work one longs for other voices, for the company of one's friends, of books. One feels one has been away from the world too long and one wants to integrate oneself with it, to 'live' again. But this is very curious. One leaves the world because one feels the need to write in order to come fully alive, and then one is glad writing is coming to an end because in the later stages it was starting to feel more like death than life. Does the act of making on which the artist is engaged bring him more fully in touch with his real self and with the world, or does it take him further away from both?

At this point I happened to read again Yeats's great poem, 'Ego Dominus Tuus'. It is a dialogue between the two parts of the self, *Hic* and *Ille*, that which is near and that which is far. The poem asks what activity leads to true self-knowledge and self-fulfilment, and it takes the form of a debate between the claims of introspection and rhetoric, meditation and the making if images. *Hic* accuses *Ille* of never facing up to himself but of always escaping into the creation of yet one more image; *Ille* defends himself by saying that meditation and introspection do not lead to true self-knowledge but only to dreamy self-satisfaction or self-laceration. The poem does not come down on either side, but only shows up the dangers and weaknesses of both. Like all true dialogues, it has no end.

But it is not just about the choices each human being and each artist has to make; it is also concerned with the contrast

xiv

between epochs, between the art of the past and that of the
present. 'I would find myself and not an image', says *Hic*,
whereupon *Ille* replies:

> That is our modern hope, and by its light
> We have lit upon the gentle, sensitive mind
> And lost the old nonchalance of the hand;
> Whether we have chosen chisel, pen or brush,
> We are but critics or but half create,
> Timid, entangled, empty and abashed...

This is the argument between Classicism and Romanticism,
between an art based on the principles of rhetoric and one
based on the principle of sincerity. One of the exciting things
about the poem is the way Yeats restates these old oppositions
in an entirely fresh way and shows that, far from belonging to
the mere history of art, the issues are as fresh and alive today as
they ever were.

Yeats's poem, as well as confirming me in my feeling that I
had a genuine subject on my hands, also alerted me to the fact
that that subject had a historical dimension. If I was going to
do it justice I would have to try and explore the assumptions
and the limitations of both the ancient rhetorical tradition and
the tradition of sincerity which replaced it with the rise of the
novel and the coming of Romanticism. This is what I have
tried to do in the second and third lectures.

Once I started work on the lectures they took on a logic of
their own, and I discovered that the real centre of debate was
not quite where I thought it was. In the end the Yeats poem
disappeared entirely and was replaced even in the epigraph,
where it had lingered almost to the end, by a quotation from
Kafka. This quotation, an entire 'story' from one of the few
collections Kafka published in his lifetime, manages in a few
lines to bring out what I finally saw to be the elusive theme for
which I had been searching from the moment I accepted the
assignment: the relations between writing and the body.

It remains to add that by the time I had finished I had learnt something else. This is that writing and thinking discursively about this subject, however, tempting it may seem while one is engaged in the process of making, is itself an unsatisfactory compromise. The maker, however much he wants to, cannot understand himself and what drives him to make; he can only be honest to his inspiration and hope history will vindicate him. This is actually the theme of the closing sections of the third and the whole of the fourth lecture. As I wrote them I realised that I was writing against myself, and that what I was arguing for was the inadequacy of the mode of argument itself. But then that is one of the miracles of language, that it allows us to do just that.

I am grateful to the Provost and Fellows of University College, London, for inviting me to give the lectures in the first place, and to Professor Karl Miller for his unfailing courtesy and kindness.

I am also immensely grateful to my audiences, and to those friends and colleagues who took time off from their own work to read what I had written and comment upon it: Rosalind Belben, David Esterly, Dan Gunn, John Mepham, Roger Moss, Tony Nuttall, Alan Sinfield, Gerry Webster, Allon White. Without them this book would have been a poorer thing. My greatest intellectual debts are to Bernard Harrison and George Craig. They read and commented on the entire typescript and gave me encouragement when the whole project seemed either impossibly ambitious or impossibly vague. Their friendship over the past fifteen years has helped to save me from the cynicism and despair which sooner or later threatens to overcome all those who venture to teach the humanities. Finally, as always, my mother read and commented on nearly every draft, and was critical and encouraging in just the right doses.

1

The Body in the Library

————————►•◄——•◄————————

1. Let me begin with a few words about the general theme
and title of these lectures.

Our bodies are, in a sense, more familiar to us than our
closest friends; and yet they are — and will remain — mysterious and unfamiliar until we part from them. They are all
we have — yet can we really be said to have them?

In these four lectures I want to try and explore these
paradoxes and to examine the role which language, writing
and books play in our lives, the lives we live with our bodies.

These are difficult matters. When I first began to think
about them I was appalled at my inability to follow through
any clear line of argument. But then I began to realise that if
this was in part a personal weakness, it was also related to
something inherent in what I was trying to say. And I realised
why I instinctively felt that I should call the lectures '*Writing
and the Body*' and not '*Literature and the Body*'. For the term
'literature' abstracts and idealises; it suggests unity, co-
herence, a subject lying there waiting to be examined. Writ*ing*,
on the other hand, suggests a process, something that is
happening; something too that is uncertain, insecure, liable to
come to a stop at any moment as the result of cramp, boredom,
despair, or any one of a hundred unforeseen circumstances.
For writing and speaking — unlike 'art' and 'literature' — are
at the crossroads of the mental and the physical, the orders of
culture and of nature.

But notice how strong is the temptation to reify, to unify.
When I say: Writing is this or that; or, Writing must be

1

opposed to literature; or, simply, these writings — I am turning writing itself into a concept, a noun, evading its verbal
force and problematic nature. To avoid such temptations — or
perhaps, as I have said, because that is the only way I myself
can work — I will proceed in these lectures not so much by way
of argument as by the exploration of certain pieces of writing.
Story and example, rather than rigorous abstract argument,
will be the order of the day.

And yet there is an argument of sorts in what I will be
saying, one which is partly historical and partly what would
probably be called phenomenological. I will not press it too
hard, but I hope it will emerge as these lectures proceed.

2.   Today I want to explore some simple and perhaps not so
simple facts about writing and reading. I have called this
lecture 'The Body in the Library' because I want to draw your
attention to what a very odd thing it is to read or write. A child,
looking at an adult engaged in either activity, is bound to feel
baffled. Apart from the movement of the hand, continual but
slight in the one case, occasional in the other, the person might
as well be dead . . . . And this brings me to the second aspect of
the title. I want to suggest that there is no clear line of
demarcation between highbrow and lowbrow literature that
our excitement at reading the title: 'The Body in the Library'
on the spine of the book, our wanting to know: Which body?
How? Why? — that these are not questions we should be
embarrassed about. On the contrary, they are central to our
quest.

3.   But first we need a specific body in a specific library.

In one of his finest stories Borges recounts an incident that is
purported to have taken place during the First World War. A
Chinese spy in England in the pay of the Germans learns that
the Allies are about to launch a bomb attack and that their
munitions are concentrated for this purpose in the French

2

town of Albert. At the same time he learns that his cover has been blown and that the dread Captain Richard Madden, an Irishman working for the English, is at his heels. If only he could communicate the name of the town to his chief before being caught. But how? 'My human voice was very weak. How might I make it carry to the ear of the Chief?' Suddenly he hits on a solution. He looks up the name 'Albert' in the telephone directory and takes a train to a nearby town, where a certain Stephen Albert lives. He finds him in the library of his house, and in the few minutes before Madden catches up with him, they talk. The conversation is metaphysical in the extreme, for Stephen Albert, it turns out, is, amazingly, a Sinologist, and one, moreover, who has cracked a famous puzzle of Chinese intellectual history. Finally, catching sight of Madden entering the garden, the Chinaman kills Albert and thus accomplishes his task: the Chief gets the message. Nevertheless, we know from the opening paragraph of the story what the protagonists do not: that the bombing of the town of Albert by the Germans made no difference to the course of history, for it only delayed the Allied attack by a few days, a delay which the history books now attribute to the torrential rains which fell at about that time. On the other hand Stephen Albert's death is, for the Chinaman, an irrevocable act for which there can be no pardon in the tribunal of his conscience.

4.   In this context it is worth remembering the old dream, revived in the Renaissance and positively haunting the seventeenth century, of a universal language, a language that would be understood at once by all and that would tell no lies. The dream never dies, and if in logical circles it reached its apotheosis in Whitehead and Russell's *Principia Mathematica* and was then dealt its death blow by Wittgenstein's *Tractatus*, it is one whose roots, I want to suggest, go much deeper than mere intellectual curiosity. We all, always, long for a language

that will take over from 'my very weak human voice'. Recall another post-Renaissance dream of total communication, Swift's description of the men of the Academy of Lagado, who carried every possible object on their backs and then instead of talking needed only to point. We laugh at the absurdity of it, but late in life Stravinsky, in an interview, recalled the incident. 'What did you mean, a moment ago, when you declared your disbelief in words?' asked the interviewer. 'Is it a question of their inexactness?' 'They are not so much inexact as metaphorical,' answered Stravinsky, and he added: 'Sometimes I feel like those old men Gulliver encounters in the *Voyage to Laputa*, who have renounced language and who try to converse by means of objects themselves.'

5. Is Borges suggesting that a communication *beyond words* can only be bought at the price of a death? And is a library without a body in it doomed to be a library of Babel?

In order to move closer to an understanding of what is at issue here I would like to look in more detail at one particular book, written in the mid-eighteenth century, but sending its roots back to the Renaissance while also pointing forward to Borges: Sterne's *Tristram Shandy*. And so that you may see at once why I have chosen this particular book, here are two passages from it. The first is from Chapter 14 of Volume III:

> It is a singular stroke of eloquence (at least it was so, when eloquence flourished at Athens and Rome, and would be so now, did orators wear mantles) not to mention the name of a thing, when you had the thing about you, *in petto*, ready to produce, pop, in the place you want it. A scar, an axe, a sword, a pinked doublet, a rusty helmet, a pound and a half of pot-ashes in an urn, or a three-halfpenny pickle pot, — but above all, a tender infant royally accoutred. — Though if it was too young, and the oration as long as Tully's second Philippic, — it must certainly

4

have beshit the orator's mantle. — And then again, if too old, — it must have been unwieldy and incommodious to his action, — so as to make him lose by his child almost as much as he could gain by it. — Otherwise, when a state orator has hit the precise age to a minute, — hid his Bambino in his mantle so cunningly that no mortal could smell it, — and produced so critically, that no soul could say, it came in by head and shoulders, — Oh, Sirs! it has done wonders. — It has opened the sluices, and turned the brains, and shook the principles, and unhinged the politics of half a nation.

These feats however are not to be done, except in those states and times, I say, where orators wore mantles, — and pretty large ones too, my brethren, with some twenty or five and twenty yards of good purple, superfine, market-able cloth in them, — with large flowing folds and doubles, and in a great stile of design. — All which plainly shews, may it please your worships, that the decay of eloquence, and the little good service it does at present, both within, and without doors, is owing to nothing else in the world, but short coats, and the disuse of *trunk-hose*. — We can conceal nothing under ours, Madam, worth shewing.

The second passage comes from Chapter 17 of Volume IV:

It is not half an hour ago, when (in the great hurry and precipitation of a poor devil's writing for daily bread) I threw a fair sheet, which I had just finished, and carefully wrote out, slap into the fire, instead of the foul one.

Instantly I snatched off my wig, and threw it perpendicularly, with all imaginable violence, up to the top of the room — indeed I caught it as it fell — but there was an end of the matter; nor do I think anything else in Nature, would have given such immediate ease...

6.   It has often been observed that the theme of castration and

impotence runs strongly through *Tristram Shandy*. The book opens with a conception which is frustrated in its natural flow, and it ends with an impotent bull. Between the desire and the act, between the act and its effects, falls the shadow. Mrs Shandy's one-track mind weakens, if it does not altogether stop, the natural flow of Walter's semen; Susannah's faulty memory leads to Tristram's being wrongly named; the events surrounding the person of Dr Slop lead to Tristram's nose being crushed in birth, and if this castration is purely symbolic, the same cannot be said for the later incident of the sash-window. And that incident is itself the result of Toby's castration, symbolic or otherwise, on the field of Namur, and his compulsive replaying of that moment on the bowling-green, which leads to Trim's taking the weights off the sash-windows to use for guns, which leads to the windows not staying up when they ought.... Nor is Walter himself exempt from the general blight: the hints are strong that all is not well with his sexual performance either.

7. What is the reason for this? 'Unhappy Tristram!' laments Walter,

> child of wrath! child of decrepitude! interruption! mistake! and discontent! What one misfortune or disaster in the book of embryotic evils, that could unmechanize thy frame, or entangle they filaments! which has not fallen upon thy head, or ever thou camest into the world...
> (IV.19)

This, we feel, comes as near to describing the book as we could get. And it makes us see that the impotence and failure which blights all the characters is *reduplicated* at the level of the narrative. Tristram sets out grandly to write his 'Life and Opinions', and what do we get? One cock and bull story after another. How often he is in despair! There are too many unfinished bits and pieces on his hands, too many loose ends

6

that refuse to be tied up, he is constantly frustrated by misadventures, such as throwing the clean copy instead of the rough into the fire, his papers getting used as hair-curlers by unknown women, and so on and so forth — or, as Swift's Grub Street Hack would say, 'Etcetera the Elder and Etcetera the Younger.' Nor can he seem to keep any story going once he has started it: Slawkenbergius's tale, his narrative of his journey to France, the story of Toby's amours — these start off well enough, but all soon peter out. And everyone else in the book seems to be afflicted with the same inability to keep going: remember Walter's impressive openings, or poor Trim's attempts at story-telling.

As everyone knows, the disease seems to have attacked Sterne as well. In the end *Tristram Shandy* itself is all digression and no straight line. And just as Tristram's nose is put together by Dr Slop with 'a piece of cotton and a thin piece of whalebone out of Susannah's stays', so the book is contrived out of an old sermon of Sterne's, the name of a character who is already only a skull in Shakespeare, some typographical tricks, and bits and pieces out of a variety of sixteenth and seventeenth century authors.

Is the book then an unmitigated disaster? The answer, of course, is that it is nothing of the sort. But to understand why it is a triumph and not a disaster, and to understand what *sort* of a triumph it is, we need to take the theme of failure and impotence, of frustration and confusion, as seriously as Tristram himself does.

Note though that the frustration and impotence are never absolute. Tristram, after all, does get born, the sash-window does not actually castrate him, what it does, it is suggested, is more to circumcise him; a novel — of sorts — does get written. We cannot ignore the pressures of impotence, but, in spite of everything, something struggles into existence where before it did not exist. Yet the book, like Tristram himself, exists only as a series of failures, of negations: it is not a straight line, it does not tell a proper story properly, it is not, perhaps, finally, either a novel or not a novel. Yet, like Tristram, it is indubitably there. What then, as the riddles have it, is *it*?

8. I want to suggest that Sterne, standing at the threshold of the modern world, recognises that the old rhetoric, which had upheld Cicero and Shakespeare, Ronsard and Spenser, will no longer work. The novel is the form of the future. But the novel too, Sterne realises, has its built-in contradictions. It is these he proceeds to make manifest.

To begin at the beginning. Robinson Crusoe, in the first paragraph of his story, tells us who he is and where he was born. If we ask him: But who are you? He will answer: 'Men call me, nay, I call myself, Robinson Crusoe.' For some, that is a sufficient answer. For others, including Sterne, it is nothing of the sort.

Kafka's letter to his father is relevant here. What Kafka is exploring in that extraordinary work is the relation of himself to his father, in an attempt to answer the question Crusoe never asks: Yes, but who is this Franz Kafka? Looked at from his father's point of view — and Kafka is adept at looking at things from the other person's point of view — he is weak, impotent, unmarried, a failure. Instead of his father's strength and confidence, his will to get on in the world, beget children, make a success of his business, use his religion cannily as a tool for security and social advancement, Kafka is filled with doubts, lacking belief in the meaningfulness of work, unable to marry, unable even to bring to a successful conclusion any writing he might wish to do. But looked at from another point of view everything changes. What is the relation between the sexual act and the child one fathers? A meaningless biological activity leads to its inevitable biological result: a child is born. All this is wrapped round and dignified with cultural signs: marriage, naming, teaching the child ones language, etc. etc.. Kafka's reluctance to marry could just as well spring from his

8

too great respect for the meaning of life and for the nature of sacrament; just as his inability to get any of his novels finished could spring from his too great respect for art and for truth. 'Why should I do it this way if I might just as well do it that way?' is not just a preliminary question. It is the first question and the last one too. For it is another way of asking: By what authority do I do what I do? Unable to find the conviction to do it by his private authority, he nevertheless cannot find an external authority to which he can unconditionally submit — and if submission is not unconditional then it is nothing.

Like all Kafka's writing, his letter to his father — which he never sent — is genuinely ambiguous. Its power and its despair spring from the same source: the author does not have the confidence even to adjudicate between the two points of view, that of his father and of himself. He can only move forever from the one to the other and back.

9.   Here now is the opening of *Tristram Shandy*:

> I wish either my father or my mother, or indeed both of them, as they were in duty both equally bound to it, had minded what they were about when they begot me; had they duly considered how much depended upon what they were then doing...
>
> *Pray, my dear*, quoth my mother, *have you not forgot to wind up the clock?* — *Good G-*! cried my father, making an exclamation, but taking care to moderate his voice at the same time, — *Did ever woman, since the creation of the world, interrupt a man with such a silly question?* Pray, what was your father saying? — Nothing.

We are here at the start of the book. Also at the moment of the creation of a child. We are reminded too of the creation of the world. But the making of a book is not at all the same thing as the making of a child. As Lévi-Strauss puts it:

[T]he horse does effectively give birth to the horse, and . . . through a sufficient number of generations, *equus caballus* is the true descendant of *Hipparion*. The historical validity of the reconstruction of the naturalist is guaranteed, in the last analysis, by the biological link of reproduction. On the other hand, an axe never engenders another axe; between two identical tools, or between two tools which are different but as near neighbours in form as one would wish, there will always be a radical discontinuity, which comes from the fact that the one has not issued from the other, but both from a system of representations.

The classic novel implies that the making of the novel and the making of the hero are one and the same. Novels are called *Robinson Crusoe, Tom Jones, Humphry Clinker, Clarissa*. Sterne too writes a novel with the name of the hero in the title; he too is determined to write in such a way that book and hero are inseparable. But, unlike his fellow-novelists, he is only too aware of the fact that the issue is problematic. Yet he is also aware of the fact that any such tidy distinction as Lévi-Strauss's simply will not hold either where works of art and not objects of use are being considered. For a book *is* in one sense produced biologically, in the same way as a laugh or a scream has biological roots. But a book is also, of course, like an axe, the issue not of biology but of a system of representations. But could the same not be said of human beings? Sterne's book is not 'about books' while those of other novelists are 'about people'. Because it takes people seriously, *Tristram Shandy* takes books seriously. Both Tristram himself and the novel, *Tristram Shandy*, hover uneasily between the two orders, of nature and of culture. That is the source of the book's humour and of its poignancy.

10. An axe has a function in the culture which produces it. What function has a novel?

Consider the end of Volume V:

> — Didst thou ever see a white bear? cried my father, turning his head round to Trim, who stood at the back of his chair: — No, an' please your honour, replied the corporal. — But thou couldst discourse about one, Trim, said my father, in case of need? — How is it possible, brother, quoth my Uncle Toby, if the corporal never saw one? — 'Tis the fact I want, replied my father, — and the possibility of it is as follows.

And Walter proceeds to show how it is done, with a sprightly demonstration of the possibilities of rhetorical *amplificatio*. We could be witnessing a dramatisation of a fragment of Erasmus's *De copia*.

There is no need to go over the benefits which a training in rhetoric gave to the great Renaissance writers, from Rabelais to Shakespeare. However, as I suggested some years ago, and as Terence Cave has recently demonstrated with marvellous skill and scholarship, the legacy of *copia* is two-fold. On the one hand it is a valuable expressive tool; on the other its very richness leads the more thoughtful writers to question its essence: If I can say anything, then what is the status of what I say? If I can talk about bears or beguines or beeswax or birth at the drop of a hat, and then go on to cats, clouds, coprophilia and cucumbers, then what is the point of talking about any of them? And, if I start, where am I to stop?

For Cicero such questions do not arise, since his rhetoric serves a specific forensic function. But for the writer who is pleading no one's cause, not even his own, the questions become insistent. Or, I should say, for some writers, since they clearly do not trouble Defoe or Richardson. But they do trouble Sterne. Indeed, more perhaps than any other writer, he makes his book out of precisely these questions. The novel form, after all, comes into being as the possibility of questioning the old assumptions about epic and genre. Sterne is merely carrying this critical tendency a little further, until the assumptions underlying the apparently innocent new form are themselves brought out into the open.

11.   The making of a work of art, in which, after all, artists pass the greater part of their lives, has, strangely, been largely occluded from our culture, though the product — the finished work — assumed a new centrality in the Renaissance, which it has really never lost. *Tristram Shandy* constantly reminds us — or rather, scarcely lets us forget — that someone is there, biting his pen, scratching his ear, throwing his wig into the air, someone alone in his study, someone who, like us, grows tired, is not always in control of his movements, forgets, gets excited, gets bored — someone is making this book that we are reading. And, as with all made objects — at least those made by men, not God or nature — it is put together out of bits and pieces, attached to each other by dint of hard work, skill, guile and sheer preservative instinct. But at the same time we are made strongly aware of the maker of this book: of his desires, choices, decisions — ultimately, of the darkness and silence out of which such decisions spring.

This is done by making the reader himself shoulder the task of the making. For this patchwork, piecemeal object, is also a mousetrap, designed to catch the reader. The more he withdraws, tries to establish himself in a safe position above the action, retreats to the safety of his seat in the library, the more enmeshed he becomes in the toils of the book. Once he has started reading this novel, there is no escape for him: he is made to give up many of the assumptions he held before he started, and the process is one not just of loss but also of discovery.

How is this done?

12.   I see three main strategies on Sterne's part, though naturally they overlap. The one most frequently commented

on is the direct address to the reader. Yet even this simple gesture involves us in something quite complicated. When Sterne peremptorily sends a female reader back to the previous chapter, our own exemption from this command (whether we be male or female) makes us fleetingly aware of ourselves as guilty of the very fault for which he is criticising her:

> I have imposed this penance upon the lady, neither out of wantonness nor cruelty, but from the best of motives;... — 'Tis to rebuke a vicious taste, which has crept into thousands besides herself, — of reading straight forwards, more in quest of the adventures than of the deep erudition and knowledge which a book of this cast, if read over as it should be, would infallibly impart with them... — But here comes my fair Lady. Have you read over again the chapter, Madam, as I desired you? (I.20)

13.   This leads us straight into the second strategy: the play on the reader's curiosity.

We don't like to admit it, but it is curiosity which drives us to reading novels — both picking them up in the first place and then reading them through to the end. And it seems to me that it is probably just the same kind of curiosity as that which makes us go on reading a letter addressed to someone else which falls into our hands, or makes us eager to listen to gossip. The satisfaction of curiosity is the chief reason for the popularity of the novel — the *new*.

Curiosity drives us forward, but its satisfaction nearly always involves disappointment. It is thus important for the novelist to keep us curious for the duration of the book, and make us believe against the odds that this time we will not be disappointed. Strangely, we are only too willing to co-operate in this confidence trick. Why?

'The reader will be content', writes Sterne at the end of the second volume, 'to wait for a full explanation of these matters till the next year, — when a series of things will be laid open which he little expects.' When Sterne says that the reader will be content, he makes us aware of the fact that we will *not* be content. He plays here with our desire for *fullness, openness*. We are not content to wait; *we want to know, now, as soon as possible*. Even more interesting is the end of Volume I:

> What these perplexities of my uncle Toby were, — 'tis impossible for you to guess; — if you could, — I should blush; not as a relation, — not as a man, — nor even as a woman, — but I should blush as an author; inasmuch as I set no small store by myself upon this very account, that my reader has never yet been able to guess at any thing. And in this, Sir, I am of so nice and singular a humour, that if I thought you was able to form the least judgement or probable conjecture to yourself, of what was to come in the next page, — I would tear it out of my book.

Though Sterne/Tristram denies that he would blush as a man, the very denial arouses our expectations, which the context reinforces: what Volume II will reveal will have something to do with Toby's sexual life. Blushing as a man and as an author then may not be such separate things; it may be that curiosity in the sense in which I have been describing it is nearly always sexual curiosity.

14.   Earlier critics, who objected to Sterne's dirty mind, are not to be lightly dismissed. The book abounds in sexual innuendos. But I think the reason is not simply or only Sterne's prurience or his realisation that such things would sell his books — though both probably played a part.

Look at this example of innuendo. Sterne/Tristram is dismissing Locke and doing one of his typical Swiftian dramatisations of a theory in order to discredit it. It is a brilliant piece of work, but part of its brilliance rests on a pretty low sort of come-on:

14

— Call down Dolly your chamber-maid, and I will give
you my cap and bell along with it, if I make not this matter
so plain that Dolly herself should understand it as well as
Malebranch. — When Dolly has indited her epistle to
Robin, and has thrust her arm into the bottom of her
pocket hanging by her right side; — take that opportunity
to recollect that the organs and faculties of perception,
can, by nothing in this world, be so aptly typified and
explained as by that one thing which Dolly's hand is in
search of. — Your organs are not so dull that I should
inform you — 'tis an inch, Sir, of red seal-wax. (II. 2)

Tristram Shandy is, among other things, a wonderful study of
the close links that exist between pornography and the novel.
Just read Slawkenbergius's tale again, or, for a more compressed form, Chapter 21 of Volume IX. The strip-tease
strategy is the same in both cases, and so ubiquitous is the
pattern in this book that we must sooner or later be led to ask:
Why cannot the thing be said straight out? For indeed it seems
that it cannot. At the slightest hint of talk of the sexual organs
we are presented with a row of asterisks — as if the one thing
this chatterbox of a book could not do was speak directly on
this point. Why?

15.   Consider Uncle Toby. He has been wounded in the groin
at the Battle of Namur, and the Widow Wadman is surely not
the only one to wonder if the word 'groin' is not perhaps a
euphemism. The idea of Toby having children is inconceivable to Walter, and, indeed, to us, not so much because of any
natural deficiency as because *he seems to be perfectly happy as he is.*
And what does he do with his time? He relives, via a model —
first a map and then, when that proves inadequate, a three-
dimensional reconstruction — he relives the moment when his
wound occurred *in order to make sense of it.* The compulsion is
obviously there — the opening of Volume II makes that clear

15

— but his way of coping with it is clearly entirely pleasurable. And we realise that, were the Widow Wadman successful in her campaign, that would be the end of Toby's game, of his innocence and of his happiness.

But Toby, like Walter, only develops to extremes one aspect of the writer's own situation. Tristram too has made *his* game out of the playful exploration of his own compulsive concerns with the primal scene, a scene of both birth and death, gain and loss. Indeed, it is as if the game could not be elaborated unless there were loss, castration; and unless that loss were coped with by being *displaced*.

We can now make a tentative stab at an explanation of the innuendo I began with, the narrator's remark that our present orators are no match for the ancients because they have nothing under their short tunics. They are, we may tentatively say, only orators *because* they have nothing under their tunics.

17. For the reader, no less than for the Widow Wadman, it becomes a matter of dire necessity to know what is under Toby's tunic. Yet that is the one thing Sterne will not tell him. And it is not just a matter of leading him on and then turning away. Sterne goes shallower than that.

Listen to this passage:

> — 'My sister, mayhap,' quoth my Uncle Toby, 'does not choose to let a man come so near her ****.' Make this dash, — 'tis an Aposiopesis. — Take the dash away, and write *Backside*, — 'tis Bawdy. Scratch Backside out, and put *Covered Way* in, 'tis a Metaphor; — and, I dare say, as fortification ran so much in my uncle Toby's head, that if he had been left to have added one word to the sentence, — that word was it.

Something extremely complicated is happening here. It is not just that we are being made aware of the fact that there is really no Mrs Shandy, no Toby, no Walter — that they are made up of rhetorical convenctions, words and letters — that is, ultimately, so many straight and curved black lines on white paper. No. The fiction is too powerful for that. It is that they are 'real people' for us by this time (we are half way through the second volume), alive for us as characters in fiction can be — *but also, suddenly, mere words.* We want to move forwards, get on with the story, inwards, to an understanding of their motives, *and we are frustrated.* Not because the fiction stops, but because, before our eyes, it turns into something else, into another kind of discourse. Or rather, since the characteristic of the classical novel is that the fiction conceals its status as discourse, we seem to move, as in a Möbius strip, from inside to outside without any apparent hiatus, and the harder we try to get back in, so to speak, the more resolutely we find ourselves shut out.

And this is characteristic of the book as a whole. The paragraph immediately following the one I have just quoted reads:

> But whether that was the case or not the case: — or whether the snapping of my father's tobacco-pipe so critically, happened through accident or anger, — will be seen in due time.

'Due time' is comforting. It is so as to have all explained in due time that we read on. But in this book time is never due. Incident is added to incident, word to word, and we seem to move further and further from meaning within a world of mere extension.

Consider the following, even more mind-boggling passage:

> — ANALOGY, replied my father, is the certain relation and agreement, which different — Here devil of a rap at the door snapped my father's definition (like his tobacco-pipe) in two, — and, at the same time, crushed the head of as notable and curious a dissertation as ever was engendered in the womb of speculation... (II. 7)

17

The definition, like the tobacco-pipe, is snapped in two. But that of course is not all. We have already had a hint of what is going to happen to Tristram's nose as he is brought into the world, though the actual incident will only be recounted later. But we are suddenly made to ask ourselves: Which engenders which, the reality the metaphor or the metaphor the reality? The answer must be that neither comes first; they lie alongside each other, affecting each other by a kind of metonymic contamination. The effect is eerie. Which is an analogy for which? Are they both perhaps analogies for something else? When we later learn of Tristram's head being crushed in his mother's womb we feel for him, putting ourselves in his place — even that place — as we always do when reading fiction — but at the same time we half-sense that this may not really be happening, that it may all be metaphor or analogy, that Tristram himself may be an analogy, and so that we too, who thought ourselves so solid, may only be... what?

18. We begin to see that our wish to get at the 'real' meaning of the book is more than a matter of idle curiosity. Perhaps curiosity is never idle. A great deal seems to be at stake for us as readers in its satisfaction. But can curiosity ever be satisfied?

> I define a nose as follows [writes Tristram] — entreating only beforehand, and beseeching my readers, both male and female, of what age, complexion and condition soever, for the love of God and their own souls, to guard against the temptations and suggestions of the devil, and suffer him by no art or wile to put any other ideas into their minds, than what I put into my definition. — For by the word *Nose*, throughout all this long chapter of noses, and in every other part of my work, where the word *Nose* occurrs, — I declare, by that word I mean a Nose, and nothing else, or less. (III.31)

But it is a characteristic of speech and writing that meaning

18

cannot simply be circumscribed in this way. If a nose is the
centre of a story we are bound to ask why. And if the answer
cannot be given in terms of verisimilitude — and even here
there is something puzzling, unaccounted for — then the thing
must have another meaning. Walter, at any rate, is convinced
of this, and a little later we find him studying Erasmus on
noses:

> Nature had been prodigal in her gifts to my father beyond
> measure, and had sown the seeds of verbal criticism as
> deep within him, as she had done the seeds of all other
> knowledge, — so that he got out his pen-knife, and was
> trying experiments upon the sentence, to see if he could not
> scratch some better sense into it. — I've got within a single
> letter, brother Toby, cried my father, of Erasmus his
> mystic meaning. — You are near enough, brother, replied
> my uncle, in all conscience. — Pshaw! cried my father,
> scratching on, — I might as well be seven miles off. — I've
> done it, said my father, snapping his fingers. — See, my
> dear brother Toby, how I have mended the sense. — But
> you have marred a word, replied my uncle Toby. — My
> father put on his spectacles, — bit his lip, — and tore out
> the leaf in a passion.

It seems to be a law here that we urgently desire to get to the
heart of meaning, yet that to get there is to mar all. Indirection
is the order of the day, in *Tristram Shandy* just as much as in *A la
recherche du temps perdu*.

19.   It is here that what I will call the collage elements —
black pages, marbled pages, asterisks, pointing fingers, even
the relative lengths of the dashes which eighteenth-century
printers were willing to supply but the use of which we have
now lost — here that what I will call the collage elements come
into play. They do not all function in precisely the same way,
of course, and it would be interesting to analyse the different

19

effects on the reader of a black and a marbled page. The invitation of the first is to go behind, to lift up the stone of the tomb and behold Yorick lying beneath, so to speak; the effect of the second is to make us trace patterns in an effort to discover meaning. Again, a pointing finger makes different demands from the twirling trajectory of a walking stick. But by and large we can say that the collage elements seem to give us the thing itself, which mere words have been unable to do. But at the same time as they give, they take away. A pointing finger remains only an icon of the human hand, its silent presence in a book even more ludicrously uninformative than words. So we hurry back from the collage elements, back to the words which will, perhaps, after all, yield up the secret — but of course they never do.

20. We can now see that the ultimate play with the reader still involves curiosity, and that this curiosity is still sexual, if we are prepared to recognise that the domain of sex is as large as Freud suggested — that is, that what is at stake is the desire to discover the meaning of one's body.

This curiosity, in Sterne, is forever being frustrated. And as this happens we come to realise that to read 'deeply' and to read 'frivolously' amount to the same thing. Both rest on the assumption that ultimately, either 'beneath' or 'in the end', there is a 'real truth' or 'real centre', which we can reach. But Sterne demonstrates that though this is a perfectly natural mistake to make, it is a mistake nonetheless: there is no Father at the start, disseminating meaning, no virile bull at the end. There is only an absence, a lack — no cock and no bull, but only a cock and bull story.

And yet that 'only', though it is in one sense an admission of failure, is also the precondition of triumph. I want now to suggest that the book's recognition of its poverty, of the way it is merely stuck together by a kind of *bricolage*, of its lack of cock — that this is not merely a sign of its greater honesty, but also that which allows it to be more than the vehicle for Sterne's 'terribly weak human voice', and to affect us where it most matters: in our very bodies.

21.   I began by reminding you of Walter's despair at what Fortune had done to make his child quite other than he might have wished. But perhaps Tristram is only the child of misfortune and disaster because Walter's expectations are so Utopian. In fact, for Walter, his son is only one more *idea*. '"Were I an absolute prince," he would say, pulling up his breeches with both hands, as he rose from his arm-chair, "I would appoint able judges..."'. But just as Gonzalo's dreams serve to define the reality of Prospero's island, so Walter's Utopian fantasies, the more they are indulged, the more they help us see the reality of the Shandy household. (And are not Defoe and Crusoe really Walters, though Walters who are indeed absolute princes on their own islands?)

In *Tristram Shandy*, the more Walter treats Tristram as a mere idea, the more Tristram's resistant corporality is borne in on us. The opening of Volume III is particularly interesting in this respect. We have got used to the fact that Tristram is not yet born — and then suddenly he is there, and we realise that he has actually been there for some time. Sterne's refusal to pander to our expectations of being present at the birth, so to speak, is rather like Proust's killing off of Swann in a subordinate clause. The continuous talk about everything under the sun that goes on while birth is taking place elsewhere in the house makes that silent (unspeakable) event present to us in ways description of it never could. Again, in the discussion of the Tristrapaedia, the excess of mere words and their lack of relation to the living child brings that child's reality poignantly home to us. As in Proust once more (a point beautifully brought out by George Craig in a recent essay), the overt direction of the pointing finger helps alert us to the silent unseen object away from which the finger points. Tristram is:

all that which is other than words, all that which his father cannot speak.

But how? you will say. Is not Tristram before us the whole time? Are not his words all that we see and hear?

Yes. But he is not an object submitted to our gaze; he is a source of potential. He is not described and defined by the words in the book; rather, he is present in and through them.

22. But could one not say this of any first person narrator? I think not.

Earlier I compared Toby's innocent games on the bowling green with Tristram's games in the study at his writing-table. Now I have contrasted Walter and Tristram. And it is true that of the two Toby is more like Tristram than Walter. But there is another sense in which both seem to exist in stark contrast to Tristram. They are types of the man of action and the scholar, and neither has any doubts about the validity of either his calling or his philosophy of life. Yet this very lack of doubt gives their lives a quite unreal air; they exist happily ensconced in their own cocoons, and neither engages with reality at any point. It is Toby whistling away what is uncomfortable, Walter talking it away, who are the children of this book, and not even the children but the babies, clinging for all they are worth to the Pleasure Principle, and perpetually denying reality. By contrast Tristram's struggles to get his book written, and even the continuing saga of the failure of Walter's ideals where he is concerned, are signs of a response to reality which can only be called creative.

To understand just why this should be so we need to understand a little more clearly the role of interruption in this novel. Walter, you will remember, described his son not just as a child of wrath and decrepitude, but as a child of interruption. And I suggested that interruption was characteristic of the novel as a whole. So far we have looked at it in its negative aspect, so to speak, as a denial of the reader's desire to move forward to a fullness of truth. Now we need to examine its positive role.

Walter Benjamin has acutely observed the function of interruption in Brecht's theatre:

> The task of epic theatre [he says] ... is not so much the development of actions as the representation of conditions. This does not mean reproduction as the theoreticians of Naturalism understood it. Rather, the truly important thing is to discover the conditions of life .... This ... takes place through the interruption of happenings .... Epic theatre is by definition a gestic theatre. For the more frequently we interrupt someone in the act of acting, the more gestures result.

Robinson Crusoe and *The Praise of Folly* are, in their different ways, comfortable works to live with. They establish a convention or distance at the start and remain faithful to it throughout the work. But *Tristram Shandy* is a story of interruptions, a story made up of multiple gestures, and that is much more exciting, amusing and disturbing.

The classic novel exists in time in ways in which even the longest epic cannot be said to do. That is, it both takes time to read and it is concerned with the passing of time. But, curiously it seems quite unable to register the actual effects of time. Or perhaps we should say that in the classic novel time exists as a beneficient deity, one who will bring forth whatever is in her womb. Its other name is plot.

Plot, in the sense in which it exists in George Eliot or Dickens, does not exist in *Tristram Shandy*. That novel's movement is all sideways, never forwards towards the final revelation inherent in plot. *Tristram Shandy* thus seems to stand in the same relation to the classic novel as, according to Benjamin's 'Theses on the Philosophy of History', historical materialism stands to historicism. This is how Benjamin puts it:

23

A historical materialist cannot do without the notion of a present which is not a transition, but in which time stands still and has come to a stop. For this notion defines the present in which he himself is writing history.

The present in the classic novel is always a transition; in *Tristram Shandy* time, as we have seen, keeps standing still, and this precisely defines the present in which the story is trying to get written. Historicism inevitably culminates in universal history, but

> Universal history has no theoretical armature. Its method is additive; it musters a mass of data to fill a homogeneous, empty time. Materialist historiography, on the other hand, is based on a constructive principle. Thinking involves not only the flow of thoughts, but their arrest as well. Where thinking suddenly stops in a configuration pregnant with tensions, it gives that configuration a shock...

When that happens the present is suddenly seen as 'the time of the now', which, says Benjamin, is 'shot through with the chips of Messianic time.'

These aphoristic formulations, terse and compressed as they are, nevertheless help us to see the source of the power of Sterne's novel. From this perspective not only the play with time but the whole bag of tricks associated with the novel take on a new significance. By interrupting an action Sterne makes us aware of the potential of actions; by fragmenting, changing direction, never allowing us to relax in a distance established once and for all between ourselves and the novel, he brings the world alive for us.

23.   Can we be more precise about this?

I have already given numerous examples of how Sterne refuses to let us settle into the comfort of accepting the book either as rhetoric or as history. We cannot read it as we do most novels, for it keeps flattening out into rhetoric (an interruption is merely an aposiopesis). On the other hand we cannot read it as a rhetorical game, for it maintains connections with lived reality, it works on us as novels always do work, bringing the characters and events alive for us as they would be were we to receive a letter about them from a friend.

The unsettling, double quality of this book is manifested most clearly in its dealings with time.

Traditional story-telling has always taken place in a special time. The community gathers round and listens to one of their number, specially gifted with memory and eloquence, who repeats for them the stories they have so often heard before. While he talks, usually in the long evening hours when it is no longer possible to work in the fields or out at sea, the women may well get on with the work of their hands, basket-weaving or rope-making, while the children fool around or drop off to sleep. In that way time passes. But time, the history of the community, is also re-affirmed, in the story and by the very gathering of its members to listen to the story. A novel, on the other hand, is read by each of us alone, in bed, in an armchair or in a library. We do nothing with our hands while we read. Our hours with the book help us to pass the time and allow us to escape from our own meaningless lives into the meaningful and purposeful life of the hero.

Sterne will have none of that. He is at pains to remind us that telling stories *takes up time*, ordinary common or garden time, and so does listening to or reading them. As in Cervantes, the action keeps breaking off while people gather round to listen to someone tell a story. But here, unlike Cervantes' novel, whose author, with one part of himself, still tries to believe that he lives in a world of oral story-telling, here there is always the sense that they should be doing something else, that the time they are spending *here* is time they are wasting *there*. And if this is true of the characters of the book, it is true,

25

willy nilly, of Tristram himself, of Sterne, and of the reader.

'I like to hear Trim's stories about the captain,' says Susannah. And then 'Susannah, the cook, Jonathan, Obadiah, and corporal Trim formed a circle about the fire; and as soon as the scullion had shut the kitchen door, — the corporal begun.' But instead of giving us the corporal's story, for which we are now as keen as the servants, the next chapter begins: 'I am a Turk if I had not so much as forgot my mother.' We too had forgotten Mrs Shandy and must, reluctantly, turn from the corporal's tale to attend to her.

Partly what this does is to reinforce the Puritan sense that it is wrong to listen to stories, that time must be used well, not idled away. ''Tis commonly observed,' wrote one reformer in 1704, 'that the first step to wickedness is idleness; and indeed there is little hopes of anyone being a good man or a good Christian, who has no care of his time.' In a chapter entitled 'Of Spending Time', in his *Advice to an Only Child* (1693), the Presbyterian Oliver Heywood offered the following typical counsel:

> Never do anything merely to pass the time away. Neither make any visits, nor set upon any thing called recreation, barely on that account. Time is too precious a jewel, too valuable a treasure, to study how to get rid of it, as some do of an old commodity that lies on their hands, that they cannot tell what to do with. God never gave us the least pittance or moment of good to trifle away...

But one does not have to invoke historical explanations. The reformers may have no doubts as to how one *should* spend one's time, but Tristram and Sterne certainly do. To begin with the novel shows us how we use stories in order to protect ourselves from the consequences of time. Remember, for example, how the assault on the Widow Wadman is delayed and delayed while Trim goes through the complicated ritual of starting a story, eagerly abetted by Toby. Both of them know that a successful assault on the Widow (and any assault on that lady is likely to be successful) will spell the end of the happy life they have lived up to then. Telling stories is an excellent way of postponing that moment.

Time spent telling stories and listening to them, time spent writing and reading, is time not spent elsewhere. And for the characters in this book elsewhere is not better but worse than here. Elsewhere is in fact the place where time passes and death is seen to come a little nearer every second.

All talk of *Tristram Shandy* as a game with the reader, a brilliant rhetorical exercise, founders on this rock. For if the book is, as I have suggested, like Toby's games, a way of deflecting sexuality and making it manageable, it is also, quite simply, an ultimately hopeless flight from death. Tristram writes for all he's worth, but there is no privileged time for writing, no chamber sealed off from time and the world in which the writer can settle at his ease. That is why Volume VII is placed where it is. It is the necessary complement to Volumes I-II and VIII-IX, the volumes which deal respectively with birth and love.

24. Volume VII brings all the issues of the book together: the nature of verisimilitude; the relations of fiction to pornography; of writing to sex and death.

The tone does not change, but that makes it all the more painful to read. Is Tristram's journey to France to try to escape Death a real journey or only a metaphor or analogy? But what does 'real' mean here? Volume VI, for example, begins:

> — We'll not stop two moments, my dear Sir, — only, as we have got through these five volumes, (do, Sir, sit down upon a set — they are better than nothing) let us just look back upon the country we have passed through. —

A common enough metaphor. But suddenly we find that this is a journey we too are embarked on, and one we cannot conveniently escape from merely by putting down the book:

> Now there is nothing in this world I abominate worse, than
> to be interrupted in a story — and I was that moment
> telling Eugenius a most tawdry one in my way, of a nun
> who fancied herself a shell-fish, and of a monk damned for
> eating a mussel, and was shewing him the grounds and
> justice of the procedure —
>
> ' — Did ever so grave a personage get into so vile a
> scrape?' quoth Death. Thou hast had a narrow escape,
> Tristram, said Eugenius, taking hold of my hand as I
> finished my story —
>
> But there is no *living*, Eugenius, replied I, at this rate; for
> as this *son of a whore* has found out my lodgings —
>
> — You call him rightly, said Eugenius — for by sin, we
> are told, he entered the world — I care not which way he
> entered, quoth I, provided he be not in such a hurry to take
> me out with him — for I have forty volumes to write, and
> forty thousand things to say and do, which no body in the
> world will say and do for me, except thyself; and as thou
> seest he has got me by the throat (for Eugenius could scarce
> hear me speak across the table) and that I am no match for
> him in the open field, had I not better, whilst these two
> spider legs of mine (holding one of them up to him) are
> able to support me — had I not better, Eugenius, fly for my
> life? 'Tis my advice, my dear Tristram, said Eugenius —
> Then by heaven! I will lead him a dance he little thinks of
> — for I will gallop, quoth I, without looking once behind
> me, to the banks of the Garonne; and if I hear him
> clattering at my heels— I'll scamper away to mount
> Vesuvius...

The writer who senses the possibilities of his craft is in
control of the reader of this book; he can play with time in it,
stop, move off in a different direction, turn round suddenly
and pounce on the reader from behind. But even as he does

that time is passing. It cannot be spoken, for to speak it is to deny it; it can only be felt. And, as I suggested we felt Tristram's presence in the area of silence which surrounds him, so we feel death as the book draws to its end, a spectral presence which had in fact been there from the start. It was this, unknown to us and to him, which led to his desperation at not being able to get his story off the ground. Now it pervades everything as, four hundred pages and so many years later, still nothing meaningful has been achieved.

25.   Plot and metaphor suggest a triumph of the artist over time. It is not surprising that aestheticians, concerned to replace religion by art, have made so much of these things. *Tristram Shandy* enacts the effort to achieve them and the failure of that effort. The book is all extension and no meaning, all analogy and metonymy and no metaphor or plot.

Writing and reading take place in time. They cannot escape it. This novel does not try to. Again, as with *A la recherche*, it temporarily frees us from the compulsion of both sex and time by making us recognise them for what they are. Though Proust flirts with a Platonic solution in *Le temps retrouvé*, in the end he remains faithful to his profoundest insight: that we are given back time by recognising that it is what inevitably passes. We are really in it, and what is happening to us is really going by as it happens, the future is not at a distance, but is always becoming the present, and there is no graspable shape to our lives except this process. To avoid recognition of this is to avoid recognition of one's own body. To accept the one is to be given back the other.

In Borges's story, with which I began, the narrator makes an amazing discovery:

Through the window I saw the familiar roofs and the cloud-shaded six o'clock sun. It seemed incredible to me that that day without premonitions or symbols should be the one of my inexorable death. In spite of my dead father, in spite of having been a child in a symmetrical garden of Hai Feng, was I — now — going to die? Then I reflected that everything happens to a man precisely, precisely *now*.

In Stephen Albert's library the other side is presented to him:

> In all fictional works, each time a man is confronted with several alternatives, he chooses one and eliminates the others; in the fiction of Ts'ui Pên, he chooses — simultaneously — all of them.... Sometimes, the paths of this labyrinth converge: for example, you arrive at this house; but in one of the possible pasts you are my enemy, in another, my friend.

It is not surprising that commentators have seized on this latter aspect of Borges at the expense of the former. That everything happens to a man precisely *now*, that death is not something I can ever tame by the use of the imagination, is not an easy notion to grasp, since to grasp it the imagination must somehow recognise its own limits. In fact, it can only be grasped by realising its opposite: because I grasp that there are alternative lives I could live, I could have lived, I am able to understand why the one I do live and have lived is necessary.

26.   In Chapter twelve of Volume I we are told of Yorick's death. We are told that he lies under a plain marble slab, upon which is inscribed the legend: 'Alas, poor Yorick!' The name is in capitals, followed by an exclamation mark, and the legend has a black line round it. A few lines later the phrase is repeated. Again it is placed on a separate line, but this time it is not bounded. We are asked to imagine the words sighingly spoken by those who pass by: 'Alas, poor Yorick!'

If we try to unpack the effect of this on us we get something like this. An epitaph may be quaint or amusing, but it has to be essentially true: 'Here lies X or Y' is something we do not friend was broke; he squeez'd his hand,——and then walk'd softly out of the room, weeping as he walk'd. *Yorick* followed *Eugenius* with his eyes to the door,----he then closed them,—and never opened them more.

He lies buried in a corner of his church-yard, in the parish of————, under a plain marble slabb, which his friend *Eugenius*, by leave of his executors, laid upon his grave, with no more than these three words of inscription serving both for his epitaph and elegy.

5

Alas, poor Y O R I C K !

Ten times in a day has *Yorick*'s ghost the consolation to hear his monumental inscription read over with such a variety of plaintive tones, as denote a general pity and esteem for him;——a foot-way crossing the church-yard close by the side of his grave,—not a passenger goes by without stopping to cast a look upon it,——and sighing as he walks on,

Alas, poor Y O R I C K !

The end of Vol. I, Ch. 12 of "Tristram Shandy"

question. But of course there is no body underneath the page we are reading. A novel is not a tomb, the words inscribed on its cover do not function in the same way as does an epitaph. On the other hand if we imagine it does, the book will indeed become a kind of tomb. Yet if we simply read it as a 'story' we will somehow miss the body which does lie behind it. What happens as we read this page of the book is that we react to the tone, a tone by turns sentimental and prurient. But the tone forces us to laugh at the absurd combination of funerary inscription and exclamation mark, at the uneasy mixture of the hieratic and the demotic, the eternal and the evanescent. And if we have doubts about the epitaph, what about the repetition of the phrase? Can it really be what people feel about Yorick? Have we not heard it somewhere before, in rather less reverential a context?

We recognise the strength of our feelings — we *want* to feel for Yorick. But we are only made aware of them because they are deflected. After all, the phrase is not Tristram's, or that of Yorick's friends, it is a quote from the most famous play in the language. So, if it is not Yorick's fate which moves us here, what is it? Is it that of Tristram, for whom we feel *through* the uneasy language? But no, it is not that either, for Tristram himself, we feel, is the product of Sterne's imagination. Ah, so it is Sterne who moves us. But who is Sterne? An eccentric eighteenth-century clergyman? Yes, but it is not he who moves us either. The Sterne we experience as we read is the Sterne who wrote — no, the Sterne who *writes*. As he writes he comes alive, and as he writes he dies a little more each day. The recognition of the latter is what makes the former possible.

By exploring the multiple possibilities, their inevitable limitations and final disappearance, Sterne returns us, his readers, to the primal world of polymorphous perversity, *and simultaneously* makes us realise that a condition of such an exploration is that such a world has gone for good and that soon we too will be no more. As he does so the dead bones of his body and of ours begin to live. It is, as far as I am concerned, the only possible resurrection.

Stephen Albert is killed that the message may be conveyed more powerfully than it could ever be through merely human speech. Tristram is born for the same reason. The seventeenth-century dream of a universal language was doomed to failure, but that other late Renaissance discovery, the novel, in the right hands, would provide such a language: not in the words, not in the story, not in the book as an object, but in the book *as it is read*: a living body.

II

Everything and Nothing

——————⊷•⊷•⊷◂——————

1.   I spoke last week about some of the implications of writing and reading fiction, and also about Sterne's nostalgia for a time before, a time when orators had something to hide under their cloaks. In Tristram's mind this golden age seems to have been associated with Yorick, and it may be that in Sterne's own mind it was associated with Yorick's creator, the writer who could so unselfconsciously have his hero exclaim: 'Alas, poor Yorick!'

It is about that writer and that golden world that I wish to speak today. I will follow the pattern of my last lecture and start with a story by Borges. This one is called 'Everything and Nothing', and it begins like this:

> There was no one in him; behind his face (which even in the poor paintings of the period is unlike any other) and his words, which were copious, imaginative, and emotional, there was nothing but a little chill, a dream not dreamed by anyone. At first he thought everyone was like him, but the puzzled look on a friend's face when he remarked on that emptiness told him he was mistaken and convinced him forever that an individual must not differ from his species.

He goes to school, grows up, marries, moves to London:

> Instinctively, he had already trained himself in the habit of pretending that he was someone, so that it would not be discovered that he was no one. In London he hit upon the

34

profession to which he was predestined, that of the actor, who plays on stage at being someone else. His playacting taught him a singular happiness, perhaps the first he had known; but when the last line was applauded and the last corpse removed from the stage, the hated sense of unreality came over him again.

So he turns to dreaming, and then to writing about the heroes of his dreams.

Twenty years he persisted in that controlled hallucination, but one morning he was overcome by the surfeit and the horror of being so many kings who die by the sword and so many unhappy lovers who converge, diverge, and melodiously agonize.... That same day he disposed of his theatre. Before a week was out he had returned to the village of his birth, where he recovered the trees and the river of his childhood; and he did not bind them to those others his muse had celebrated, those made illustrious by mythological allusions and Latin phrases. He had to be someone; he became a retired impresario who has made his fortune and who interests himself in loans, lawsuits, and petty usury...

The story goes that, before, or after he died, he found himself before God and he said: 'I who have been so many men in vain, want to be one man: myself.' The voice of God replied from a whirlwind: 'Neither am I one self; I dreamed the world as you dreamed your work, my Shakespeare, and among the shapes of my dream are you, who, like me, are many persons — and none.'

Perhaps we feel that this is slightly sentimental; yet Borges has, I think, touched on a central factor in our experience of Shakespeare. He is not, like the nineteenth-century Shakespearians, trying to give us a spiritual biography of the

dramatist; rather, like Coleridge and Ruskin, he is high-
lighting what Frank Kermode has called Shakespeare's
patience, his ability to absorb all our questions. Indeed,
Kermode, at the end of his fine centennial lecture called
'The Patience of Shakespeare', quotes from a poem by
Delmore Schwartz which ends in a very similar vein to
Borges's story:

> . . . sweet prince, black night has always descended and
> has always ended.
> . . . prince of Avon, sovereign and king
> With all the sweetness and all the truth with which you
> sang anything and everything.

2.   It is not difficult to recognise the truth of such remarks;
but it is difficult to know where to go, critically, from there. We
don't seem to have the critical vocabulary to deal with the
notions of patience and allied concepts. Our critical vocabulary directs us to open up, explore, understand. The criticism
of Shakespeare which wants to go in a different direction is
usually reduced to the reiteration of platitudes.

No one has done more to help us break out of this impasse
than Northrop Frye. In his marvellous lectures on the
comedies, *A Natural Perspective*, he points out that

> It is curious that we can think of impartiality only as
> detachment, of devotion to craftsmanship only as purism,
> an attitude which, as in Flaubert, turns all simple life into
> an enormously intricate still life, like the golden touch of
> Midas. We can hardly conceive of an imagination so
> concrete that for it the structure is prior to the attitude,
> and prescribes the attitude. Shakespeare's impartiality is a
> totally involved and committed impartiality; it expresses
> itself in bringing everything equally to life.

This is a vitally important insight, and I will return to it from a different angle in the next lecture. But it is not an easy notion to grasp, so let us try to follow Frye as he fleshes it out.

'Of course all art is conventionalised,' he says, 'but where the convention is most obvious and obtrusive the sense of play, of accepting the rules of the game, is at its strongest.' For Shakespeare 'does not ask his audiences to accept illusion: he asks them to listen to a story.' In this he is quite different from Jonson, who wants to teach and correct, and who 'strives in his art to create an unbreakable illusion.' Frye suggests that 'Shakespeare's plays bring us close to the oral tradition, with its shifting and kaleidoscopic variants, its migrating themes and motifs, its tolerance of interpolation, its detachment from the printed ideal of an established text.' He points out that in Jonson the complexity of the drama tends to be teleological, directed towards an end in which all will be resolved, while in Shakespeare it is often processional and contrapuntal. If we think of the miracle plays, of *Tamburlaine*, we see that English drama before Jonson tends towards the processional, and that Shakespeare never loses his fondness for this right up to *Henry VIII*.

What all this suggests to Frye is that if we see the comedies rather than the tragedies as central to Shakespeare's output, then he is found to have affinities with older and non-Western drama and with opera, whereas Jonson initiates a tradition which is still dominant today, though less obviously so than in the nineteenth century, the tradition of what we might call the well-made play. Frye reminds us of Chinese plays of the Sung period, which cannot readily be distinguished from opera, for music plays a crucial role in them, keeping the *plot* always subordinate to the *rhythm*: 'Plots of operas are often more uninhibited than plots of plays, because the driving force of the opera is provided by the music.' Thus

In *Figaro* we have a comfortable feeling that no doubt all the complications will work out as they should, but in the meantime something more important, like 'Voi che Sapete' or 'Dove sono' is likely to turn up at any time and claim our main attention.

It is thus to *Figaro* and *The Magic Flute* that Frye turns when looking for parallels to *Twelfth Night* and *The Tempest*, and to operatic terms when trying to describe individual works, remarking perceptively about *Pericles*, for example, that

> Gower provides a narrative continuity, like *recitativo*, while the main action dramatizes the central episodes. In the imagery music is practically the hero of the play: it is to the action of *Pericles* what Prospero's magic is to the action of *The Tempest*

3. Frye's insistence on the story-telling elements in Shakespeare, on his affinities with medieval drama, Chinese music-drama and opera seems to me wholly justified and very illuminating. And anyone who reads through the thirty-six plays is bound to feel that Shakespeare is here exploring the possibilities of dramatic form in very much the same way as Bach and Mozart explored the possibilities of the musical forms they inherited. 'Then learn this of me,' Touchstone says to William, 'To have is to have; for it is a figure in rhetoric that drink, being poured out of a cup into a glass, by filling the one doth empty the other.' Shakespeare pours from cup to glass to mug, but the cup is always full, for we are in a world where giving only makes us discover how much we have. That is why our pleasure in him is so immeasurably enhanced when we start to become familiar enough with his plays to note the repetitions and permutations. And here I am not thinking only of the storms at sea, identical twins, heroines disguised as boys, retreats into forests and disappearing rulers. I am thinking also of the way contrasts emerge more sharply through our awareness of similarity. Thus, to take *Othello* as a purely arbitrary focus, we note that both Iago and Macbeth are described as

'honest' when we first meet them, but with Iago it is a plain case of mistaken identity, while with Macbeth it is at least partly true. And we may wonder whether, if Iago and not Othello had been the centre of the dramatist's attention, we might not have discovered the same to be true of him. Again, Othello and Leontes have much in common, but where all Shakespeare's skill goes into motivating the jealousy of the former, having done that he now wants to focus on the aftermath of jealousy and so makes the motivation as perfunctory as possible. Or, if we see Iago as a manipulator, organising the action, and Othello as a slow-speaking, clumsy, good-hearted non-European who is taught a new kind of language by Iago in which curses figure prominently, we may suddenly feel that we are not all that far from the Prospero-Caliban relationship.

These examples, however, perhaps alert us to an unease we may feel with Frye's argument. Profound and salutary as it is, it is noticeably more successful in dealing with the comedies than with the tragedies. And you will I am sure have noted too that it only takes up one aspect of Borges's little story. For what Borges suggests of course is that the very strengths we have been outlining are also, for Shakespeare, a source of deep anxiety. Borges would not be justified in making this claim — or rather, we would not register it as at least partly true — if it were not for the fact that Shakespeare himself seems concerned with it. For what else is *Richard II* but a play which explores the relationship of what a man says and does to what he is? And *Hamlet* of course derives a large part of its power from the fact that it dramatises the very dilemma with which Borges is concerned: Who am I? What is the relationship between myself and the roles I am called upon to play? What action is the right action? What is the right way for *me* to die?

Shakespeare, I suspect, holds the place he does in our literature — and our affections — just because he both exists in the same world as the Sung dramatists and the writers of the miracle plays, and because he is close enough to the decline of that world to ask himself questions about it. In that he is like Mozart, who also holds an ambiguous and pivotal position in the history of his art.

But it is not just a matter of *when* Shakespeare and Mozart lived and worked. It is not just that Mozart is more classical than Beethoven, more romantic than Haydn, or Shakespeare more medieval than Milton, more modern than Spenser. It has something to do with the fact that, facing as they do in both directions they seem to be aware of the *cost* of committing themselves wholeheartedly to either. Milton and Beethoven seem so confident of the rightness of what *they* have to say: Haydn and Spenser seem so confident of what they have to *do*. But Borges's story — like Kierkegaard's essay on *Don Giovanni* — is disturbing because it hints at an ambivalence at the heart of Shakespeare. Frye is right to see that compared to Jonson Shakespeare is an upholder of the old, oral, story-like kind of play, where Jonson is moving towards a new, teleologically oriented drama, with an insistence on plot and on the creation of an unbreakable illusion. But Frye perhaps does not appreciate enough what the tension between the two forms is, or how difficult it is for 'story' to survive the temptations of 'plot'.

But if Shakespeare wrote *everything*, he must have written this as well. I would like to suggest that he did, and that we find it in the play of his that comes closest to a well-made nineteenth-century drama, *Othello*.

4.   Before turning to *Othello*, however, I would like to glance very briefly at a slightly earlier play which seems to be intimately connected with it, *Twelfth Night*. This will also help us to see that our sense of Shakespeare's plays as being like the *Art of Fugue* or the *Goldberg Variations* should not, as it too easily can, be taken as implying purely formal variations and transpositions.

Twelfth Night is an ideal example of what Frye means by 'a totally involved and committed impartiality', by the sense of play being at its strongest where the conventions are the most intrusive. It is a play in which everyone plays, and those to whom our sympathies go out are those who are most aware of the game they are playing and are least concerned to establish a self in the face of the world: Feste and Viola. On the other hand Olivia, Orsino, Sir Andrew and Malvolio, in roughly descending order, exhibit the vices of these virtues, and the play demonstrates with wonderful virtuosity the errors of self-regard and the need for a willingness on the part of each of us to play the roles life requires of us in full awareness of what we are doing, without self-pity or self-seeking.

Yet to put it like this is to put it far too blandly. As always with any commentary on the comedies, one loses the speed and lightness, the breathtaking assurance of the thing itself. As Terence Cave has recently pointed out, what makes it so difficult to talk about Shakespeare is that the plays are quite prepared to comment on themselves and alert us to their reliance on convention, but such comments are themselves part of the convention. Cave concludes a discussion precisely of *Twelfth Night* by remarking:

> If one wanted to invent an allegorical schema for its inter-pretation, one might say that *Twelfth Night* dramatizes various kinds of misreading. Those characters who are deceived by the parade of figures, or who are devoted to the literal sense (which may well amount to the same thing), are misled and, according to their status, mildly teased and chastised or mercilessly baited.

However, he is quick to point out,

> This reading is itself, no doubt, a misreading; but that only serves to make more palpable the fact that the play is resistant to critical formalization. For all its linguistic and theatrical self-consciousness, *Twelfth Night* provides few

41

openings for critical discourse to begin its work; and those openings may themselves prove deceptive, so that the critic risks finding himself in the middle of the stage, smirking and sporting his yellow stockings and cross-garters for the amusement of the public.

This modest conclusion is actually, of course, a critical gain. And yet may not even this refusal of the critic to rest in any one position be itself a position of rest? Or, to put it another way, may not our placing of ourselves with such certainty *above* Malvolio be itself an example of a Malvolio-type of attitude?

Frye had noted that Shakespeare 'seems never to have addressed his audience with any other attitude than that expressed in the last line of *Twelfth Night*: "We'll strive to please you every day."' This may be true, yet neither we nor Shakespeare can forget the very real horror and humiliation to which Malvolio has been subjected: shut up in darkness and told he is mad — the ultimate nightmare of solipsism. *His* last words, we recall, are: 'I'll be revenged on the whole pack of you!'

Othello could well be called *Malvolio's Revenge*.

5. 'I look down towards his feet — but that's a fable.' Yet Iago, if not the Prince of Lies himself, is very like him. For, like the serpent in Eden, he brings division where before there was none; and he does so simply by speaking the way he does. For if language is the prerogative of man, part of its mystery lies in the fact that it can also be used against his humanity. And from the very first scene of the play we see Iago using language apparently neutrally (just as the serpent merely asked: 'Yea, hath God said, Ye shall not eat of every tree of the garden?'), but in actual fact sowing discord; waking our buried dreams and fears and then using them for his own ends.

Everyone knows the opening lines of *Twelfth Night*. The first words of *Othello*, if less memorable, are just as significant:

Roderigo:	Tush! Never tell me?...
Iago:	'Sblood, but you'll not hear me!
	If ever I did dream of such a matter,
	Abhor me.

We are used to being told things at the start of a play. In scene two of *The Tempest* Miranda notoriously does nothing but ask leading questions. Here too Roderigo seems to be asking for information, and Iago supplying it, *for our benefit*. But this is not in fact what is going on. We grasp that what has happened just prior to the opening of the play is that Iago has refused to say something. And this initial stance of blockage is one we will grow familiar with in the course of the play. It is Iago's chief ploy.

Let us examine it a little more closely. I entertain a visitor in my room. There are two doors, the one through which he has just come, and another, in the opposite wall. He may, at slack moments in our conversation, wonder where this second door leads, but the question will remain latent for him — unless, that is, I back up against it and say: 'I'm sorry, you can't go through that door.' It doesn't need Freud to explain that that 'can't' has introduced the possibility of 'can', which did not exist before that moment.

So it is with Iago. 'I will not speak,' he keeps asserting, and then, when pressed, "All right then, if you insist...'. But why should he speak in the first place? There are two sorts of answer. The first is: 'Because he wants to achieve his ends and speech is his chief weapon.' The second is: 'Because in a play everyone must speak.' When someone doesn't, on stage, this is so curious a state of affairs that it becomes the centre of the plot and the play is called *The Silent Woman*. The two answers, it will be seen, treat the work from two quite different perspectives. The first remains within the fiction of the play while the second stands back from it and looks at the dramatist's role in the presentation of that fiction. *Othello*, as we will see, forces these

43

two perspectives into far greater tension than plays which overtly try to relate them, such as *Hamlet* and *The Tempest*.

But to return to that first scene. Roderigo and Iago approach Brabantio's house and Iago suddenly breaks the silence of the night with a shout: 'Awake! What ho, Brabantio! Thieves, thieves, thieves! Look to your house, your daughter, and your bags!' The comic mode of lovers escaping the jurisdiction of the heavy father is here inverted — not just *Twelfth Night* but *The Merchant of Venice* stands behind *Othello* as its ironic mirror. Iago's call, moreover, will ring through the seventeenth century: not look *at*, but look *to*.

And what does Iago say when Brabantio appears? 'Are your doors locked?' The question, which, with variations, is the one he will plague Othello with, is the crucial one, splitting as it does inner and outer, public and private, bringing, like the serpent's question to Eve, a sense of division in what had previously been the smooth envelope of reality. But Iago has many weapons in his armoury. When Brabantio answers: 'Why, wherefore ask you this?' he is ready for him:

> Zounds, sir, Y'are robbed! For shame. Put on your gown! Your heart is burst, you have lost half your soul. Even now, now, very now, an old black ram Is tupping your white ewe.

We talk too easily perhaps about the richness of Shakespeare's language. It is, of course, overwhelming. Virginia Woolf, no mean user of language herself, jotted down in her diary:

> I never yet knew how amazing his stretch and speed and word coining power is, until I felt it utterly outpace and outrace my own, seeming to start equal and then I see him draw ahead and do things I could not in my wildest tumult and utmost press of mind imagine. Even the less known and worser plays are written at a speed that is quicker than

44

anybody else's quickest; and the words drop so fast one can't pick them up.... Evidently the pliancy of his mind was so complete that he could furbish out any train of thought; and, relaxing lets fall a shower of such unregarded flowers. Why then should anyone else attempt to write. This is not 'writing' at all. Indeed, I could say that Shakespeare surpasses literature altogether, if I knew what I meant.

Yet I think Eliot was right to be worried by Shakespeare's ease with language, and to contrast his way of writing (with just a hint of disapproval) with Dante's economy and directness. But the point is that Shakespeare too is worried by it, and *Othello* is his most significant examination of its implications. It is the measure of his greatness that he needed to understand all the implications of the extraordinary instrument at his command. Starting his career by imitating the bombast of Peele and Marlowe, he very quickly came to see that the best way to master it was to parody it, as he does in *Love's Labour's Lost* and *Henry IV*. Yet there is always a kind of safety in parody. By the time we get to *Othello* everything is in question.

For it is not of course just the *misuse* of language that is at issue. The responsible writer will see that he cannot be complacent about *any* use of language. For language, to repeat, is never neutral. To make sense of the world we have to impose a pattern upon it; to speak is to make as well as to report. And very quickly we see what kind of a pattern Iago is imposing: 'You are one of those,' he tells Brabantio, 'that will not serve God if the Devil bid you.... You'll have your daughter covered with a Barbary horse.' Even if this is not actually or even metaphorically true, it awakens echoes in the father: 'This accident is not unlike my dream. Belief of it oppresses me already.' Iago can be sure that whatever door he insists he will not open will be forced by his interlocutors, whatever image he ventures will find an echo in their dreams. Before he arrived, of

WRITING AND THE BODY

course, the doors stayed shut, the dreams remained inside the dreamers' heads.

Writing about the opening scene of *The Winter's Tale*, A. D. Nuttall makes an excellent point:

> The psychoanalyst's sense of a latent ambiguity in the childhood of Leontes and Polixenes, in the sociable affect of Hermione, is, I think, really present in the play. Yet to stress this aspect is to falsify; or at least, to distort, since it transforms what is essentially background into foreground.

Othello, I am suggesting, is a play which is primarily *about* such falsification and distortion.

6.   We have had Othello described to us in that first scene as 'thick-lips', and the insulting epithet, suggesting not only African origins but a kind of slowness and clumsiness of speech, at once imposes a contrast with Iago's speed of delivery and ability to change direction with the wind. And as Iago's opening words immediately give us the essence of his character, so it is with Othello: ''Tis better as it is,' he says when we first see him, and indeed it would be, but neither Iago nor the playwright can leave things as they are; both are committed to turning 'is' into 'becomes'.

Throughout the second scene we seem to be in quite a different world from that of the first, and it is one projected in large part by Othello's language: 'My services...shall not out-tongue his complaints.' 'I fetch my life and being From men of royal seige...' 'I would not my unhous'd free condition Put into circumscription and confine For the sea's worth.' And, finally, 'Keep up your bright swords, for the dew will rust them.' Notice the slowness of the speech, in contrast to Iago's. Silence is a crucial part of Iago's language, but it is a silence which hides what should be spoken. With Othello on the other hand, the silences come between the words, they are that out of which the words naturally spring and to which they return: they are his body, the totality of his being.

Othello, stopping the brawl, does not shout: 'Stop!' It is as if he senses that his authority externalises itself in the deliberate quality of his words. We do not think of this as rhetoric or excess, merely as the action of his character in the public sphere. 'Were it my cue to fight, I should have known it Without a prompter,' he answers Brabantio, and we respect his authority. Iago's authority lies in what he knows: Othello's in what he is. This, of course, is an effect Shakespeare works for, and it is reinforced in the following scene, partly by the deference shown Othello by the other senators, partly by Desdemona's own response to him, partly by his great speeches in his defence. Othello, it is interesting to note, has no soliloquies — how could he have, since he exists in the public world and sees himself not as a subjectivity to be explored (like Richard II and Hamlet, who have both been prized loose from the public world and forced back on themselves), but as the doer of deeds which may be recounted?

> Most potent, grave and reverend signiors...
> Rude am I in my speech...
> And little of this great world can I speak
> More than pertains to feats of broil and battle;
> And therefore little shall I grace my cause
> In speaking for myself. Yet, by your gracious patience,
> I will a round unvarnished tale deliver
> Of my whole course of love — what drugs, what charms,
> What conjuration, and what mighty magic...
> I won his daughter.

His way of speaking in his own defence is to tell a tale. And it is through tales that he won Desdemona. He told her the story of his life, not his feelings or ideas. Othello, no less than Odysseus or any other hero from oral culture, is more than he understands, is what he can *relate*.

But this is just what Iago cannot stand. For him it seems to be an evasion, an attempt to beautify and dignify human affairs 'with bombast circumstance'. For Iago ''Tis in ourselves that we are thus or thus. Our bodies are our gardens, to the which our wills are gardeners.' For him, as for Edmund in *Lear*, we are alone in a hostile world, but if we can recognise this and are not fooled by men's rhetoric, we can make sure we remain in charge of our own destinies and eventually get to the top. Thus he urges Roderigo to cheer up and put money in his purse, for 'If sanctimony and a frail vow betwixt an erring barbarian and a supersubtle Venetian be not too hard for my wits and all the tribe of hell, thou shalt enjoy her.' Othello tells a tale: Iago sums up the characters of others, like a novelist, in two words: 'erring barbarian'; 'supersubtle Venetian'.

Indeed, like the curious reader of novels, of whom I spoke in my last lecture, Iago's motive, as it emerges from the plethora of contradictory indications with which he presents us, is simply this: the need to bring things to an end, to have done with the uncertainty and multiple possibilities of life and arrive at the ultimate 'truth' of death and destruction. 'There are many events in the womb of time, which will be delivered,' he remarks, and, at the end of the first Act, in the soliloquy which is evidently *his* rightful medium:

> The Moor is of a free and open nature
> That thinks men honest that but seem to be so,
> And will as tenderly be led by th'nose
> As asses are.
> I have't! It is engendered! Hell and night
> Must bring this monstrous birth to the world's light.

7. With our analysis of the first scenes behind us, it is hardly necessary to spend very much time on how Iago succeeds in poisoning Othello's mind. It is worth noting though how the

first scene of Act II reinforces our sense of Othello's epic quality. This is the storm scene with which Verdi starts his opera. What Verdi cannot do of course, since he does not dream of taking the radical step of making Iago's a non-singing part, is to differentiate between the two men at a fundamental level. As a result his opera, for all its flamboyance, remains mere melodrama, a story of treachery, jealousy and death.

In this opening scene of Act II Othello's arrival in Cyprus is heralded by Cassio with at least two speeches which make one feel that Shakespeare must have read Homer in Greek, or at least suggest that he must have been able to intuit the authentic epic voice through paraphrase and translation by means of an imaginative sympathy which it is hard for us, in our more literate and bookish age, to understand:

> O, let the heavens
> Give him defense against the elements,
> For I have lost him on a dangerous sea!

And:

> Great Jove, Othello guard,
> And swell his sail with thine own powerful breath,
> That he may bless this bay with his tall ship.

The last line in particular, though it may not have any precise parallels in Homer, has the authentic Homeric feel. Its significance is enhanced by being followed by two scenes in which the contrast between Iago and Othello is re-emphasised.

John Bayley, in a brilliant essay on the play which in many ways forestalls and complements my own remarks, has pointed out how Iago's playful verses on women already feel as though they belonged to the narrower and more cynical world of the eighteenth century. But he does not stress enough, I feel, how profoundly shocked we are when we hear Iago reciting these verses and more especially when, a little later, he pretends to be drunk and 'breaks out' into song. My hesitation over how to describe his action suggests what is wrong. For the unspoken rule for such verses and songs is that they shall be *impromptu*, 'from the heart'. In his comedies Shakespeare has great fun parodying the verses of lovers, but we never doubt the sincerity, only the depth of feeling and technical skill, of those who produce such verses. And the power of music and song, throughout Shakespeare, rests on the fact that it is *natural*, that it springs directly from the occasion, even if, as is so often the case, it is in counterpoint to it. A song is listened to by a group gathered on stage, and by an audience in the theatre, and it binds the two groups together. It is, in some sense, public property, transcending the individual as does an oral tale. Song in Shakespeare has something of the same role as the chorus in Greek tragedy; it distils a mood and sends it over the rest of the play. Kierkegaard, writing about *Don Giovanni*, made the important point that Mozart has an inestimable advantage over Molière, in that he can use music to diffuse all that the Don stands for, the 'triumph of the musical erotic', over the whole action, in a way which Molière, with only the resources of the spoken language at his disposal in *Don Juan*, can never do. Shakespeare's Fools, drunken porters and songs make of his plays something closer to the drama of Aristophanes or the opera of Mozart than to the works of Molière or Ibsen. But Iago's is a private, anti-social nature, and the effect of hearing him break into a song is profoundly disturbing and divisive, more painful even than the experience of hearing the Pardoner, in *The Canterbury Tales*, starting to tell his own manipulative tale — more painful because we are physically present and literally hear Iago sing.

8.   Between these two episodes comes one of even greater significance, since it heralds a scene which will later prove to be the turning point of the play. Having put together his little 'Augustan' poem, Iago stands back from the action and

comments upon it as he watches Desdemona and Cassio talking together:

> He takes her by the palm. Ay, well said, whisper! With as little a web as this will I ensnare as great a fly as Cassio. Ay, smile upon her, do! I will gyve thee in thine own courtship...

We need to examine this little scene rather closely, for much hangs on our understanding of how it is affecting us. We are watching a play, *Othello*. But inside that play we are now watching another play, or rather, we are watching a dumb show and chorus such as we find in *Hamlet* (remember Ophelia's 'You are as good as a chorus my lord') and *Pericles*. But where we have no doubts about the authority of the chorus in these two plays, the situation here is rather different. For one thing, it is not of course strictly speaking a play or dumb show within the play: Desdemona and Cassio may be playing a game, but it is the game of good manners, not a play for an audience. At the same time of course they *are* playing for an audience, the audience which has come to watch *Othello*. But let us stay within the fiction for the time being and explore the implications of what is happening.

There is, first of all, no way for us to know what is *really* going on between the two. Nor is there any way for us to tell if Iago *really* thinks there is something between them, because this is how his mind works, or simply makes use of appearances for his own ends. But the point of the episode is more difficult to grasp than this (intellectually at least, for I believe it comes through quite clearly at an instinctive level in performance). It is that Desdemona and Cassio may not themselves know 'what is going on'. One way of accommodating this is to say: they may think they are merely conversing courteously, but unconsciously they are attracted to each other; or, they may think they are merely conversing courteously, but unconsciously Cassio is attracted to Desdemona; or, just possibly, they are not in the least attracted to each other, they are just going through the social rituals expected of them. (Note that a novelist would find it difficult to avoid opting for one or the other of these explanations.)

But let us pause for a moment and ask whether we think, not of other people, but of ourselves in such clear-cut ways. The answer, I think, is no. And yet the matter is complicated by the fact that we probably feel guilty for not doing so. The trouble with our culture, which tries to live according to the ethics of sincerity and feeling is that, without realising it, it is committed to notions of 'truth' and 'reality' underlying actions and events. There is a little Iago in all of us, perpetually asking: Is this *really* altruism? Surely you are being hypocritical! And so on. The Elizabethan age was still a period when people instinctively felt that human beings could not be understood in this way. They sensed that emotions could not be treated as self-subsistent real objects, but could only be defined in terms of public frames of reference. Hence the role of ritual and decorum, in life as in art. For a ritual acknowledges the complexity and indefinability of emotions and so establishes social channels for them. It is necessary to celebrate marriage, for example, with all due ceremony, because that turns the private and personal into the public and social and creates reasons for the couple to remain together regardless of the vagaries of the heart.

Ritual and rhetoric go together, though to define their relationship would take more skill, learning and time than I possess. On the other hand the realism of the novel is destructive of ritual. Ritual 'brings distance to life' in the words Walter Benjamin used about friendship; the novel abolishes distance. *Othello* stands poised between the two, dramatising the clash between them. The realism of the play has this effect on us: we see something in front of us on stage, and because it is part of a play, not part of the cotinuum of life, we feel that it means something, that we must interpret it. But to interpret is to say: this is what is *really* happening, this is what they are *really* doing. And by putting it this way we are already playing Iago's game.

We see this clearly at the end of this very scene, when Iago and Roderigo go back in conversation over what they — and we — have just seen. Iago explains to Roderigo that Desdemona is hot for Cassio, 'her eye must be fed', she has quickly tired of the Moor, and now longs for the handsome captain. 'I cannot believe that in her,' says the bewildered Roderigo. 'She's full of most blessed condition.' 'Blessed fig's end!' retorts Iago. 'The wine she drinks is made of grapes... Blessed pudding! Dids't thou not see her paddle with the palm of his hand? Dids't thou not mark that?' 'Yes, that I did; but that was but courtesy.' 'Lechery, by this hand!' snarls Iago. 'An index and obscure prologue to the history of lust and foul thoughts.'

Is Roderigo right? Or is Iago? We too have seen the episode, and how do we adjudicate? Courtesy is too weak a concept to stand up for long against the idea of lechery. Or rather, courtesy is not a concept but part of the fabric of life, of a life where public and private are not set up against each other. But of course, as the religious history of the sixteenth century shows, once the idea has taken hold that the outer is merely outer, covering an 'inner' truth, then it is impossible to return to earlier views of man. He who would assert the validity of the outer can now only do so in a despairing Swiftian way, asserting that happiness 'is a perpetual possession of being well deceived.'

In this little scene between Iago and Roderigo we can see the struggle between the two cultures, what we might call the culture of story and decorum and that of plot and truth, played out by two people who are certainly not conscious of the full implications of what they are saying and doing.

9. This prepares us, of course, for the two great temptation scenes. As John Bayley has noticed, the first of these begins in

that empty time when Desdemona is leaving the stage and Othello's thoughts are following her, though he himself remains on stage before us.

As the scene opens Cassio exits and Iago remarks, in one of his pretended asides: 'Ha! I like not that.' Othello is still distracted: 'What dost thou say?' 'Nothing, my lord...'. But, as we have repeatedly seen, to say 'nothing' is quite different from not saying anything, for nothing already conjures up a 'something' which it is negating. When Othello asks if it wasn't Cassio leaving, Iago has already won: 'Cassio, my lord? No, sure, I cannot think it, That he would steal away so guilty-like, Seeing your coming.' But we ourselves have seen Cassio and seen that there was nothing guilty about the way he left. Or was there? How *did* he look? Once an action is taken out of its place in the continuum it becomes unnatural — it becomes, that is to say, guilty.

But Iago, as we have seen, does not work only by negatives. As with Brabantio, so here, he is master of the vivid unsettling image. 'Lie — ' 'With her?' asks Othello. 'With her, on her, what you will.' 'Lie with her? Lie on her?' Othello can only gasp back at him. By the middle of the scene he is practically speaking Iago's language, a language of fluid prose, dominated by notions of cause and effect, full of violent imagery. The rest, from Iago's point of view, is simple. We can almost predict it. Once again we watch a scene in dumb show, and once again we receive the ultimate shock of being forced to watch Iago simulating passion:

> Witness, you ever-burning lights above,
> You elements that clip us round about,
> Witness that Iago here doth give up
> The execution of his wit, hands, heart
> To wronged Othello's service!

10.   Let us stand back from the play for a moment and

consider two things. The first is this. In classical tragedy, as we know, the dramatists choreographed their plays and wrote the music as well. In Asian drama what an actor did with his hands, how he sat down and stood up — all this was prescribed by tradition. To some extent the same must have been true of the miracle plays, or rather, since the important thing about these was the story they were telling, and the playing area was so restricted, the action itself must have been minimal, reduced to a few stylised gestures. But on the new open space of the Elizabethan stage, who was to say how a person should enter or exit, stab a king or beat a slave? No doubt, by the time of *Othello*, certain conventions had been established, but these were essentially ad hoc practical solutions. Shakespeare, who would leave nothing unexplored, turned, in *Othello*, to exploring the validity of this as well. What does it mean to exit from the stage? What does it mean for an audience to interpret in one way rather than another so simple an action as walking away? It is a subject he would pursue into his final plays.

The second point has to do with the issues raised by Eric Havelock in his *Preface to Plato*. Classical scholars have not all been convinced by Havelock's thesis that in Plato we see the triumph of the new, literate mentality, over the old oral culture of Homer. But Havelock, it seems to me, like Nietzsche before him, does at least present us with a paradigm of what might occur when there is such a clash. In *Othello* Shakespeare gives us his version, and, as Nietzsche suggested, he makes clear how vulnerable the oral culture is to the other. Shakespeare goes out of his way to suggest the play's links with an older, oral culture. The handkerchief is given to Othello's mother by an African witch: Desdemona sings a song once sung by her maid, Barbary; Venice, we are never allowed to forget, is Europe's window on the Orient. And, even in the midst of his conversion to Iago's way of seeing and talking, Othello still keeps reverting to his old ways: 'But yet the pity of it, Iago! O Iago, the pity of it, Iago.' And when he confronts

Desdemona he can still, like Ulysses, only think of his life in terms of a story to be told: 'I took you for that cunning whore of Venice That married with Othello.'

11.   This perhaps helps to resolve some of the problems that have notoriously beset the interpretation of the end of the play. Iago ends, as we would expect him to, asserting his privacy, that hollow centre to which others are drawn as to a magnet, and from which he will forever exclude them: 'Demand me nothing. What you know you know. From this time forth I never will speak word.' But, just as the play is seemingly all wrapped up (it could be a comedy except for that corpse on stage), Othello stops them: 'Soft you! a word or two before you go.' And then he picks himself up, rediscovers himself as a being in action, so to speak:

> I pray you in your letters,
> When you shall these unlucky deeds relate,
> Speak of me as I am.

But what is he? He does not want them to speak of him as *being* this or that — black ram or mighty warrior. He wants them to *relate a deed* — the deed he proceeds to enact before them, killing himself as he tells how he killed another. In an extraordinary metamorphosis, suicide, which in the Christian culture to which Othello in that very moment insists that he belongs (since he implicitly contrasts himself with the 'circumcised dog' he once slew) — suicide, which is seen as the ultimate sin of pride, a final denial of the self which Christ could still redeem — suicide is here made to seem a final affirmation of the self, a final act in the public sphere (Desdemona was strangled far from the gaze of all), which will allow Othello to escape at last from Iago's net. And, as if to confirm this, the last words of the play are indeed spoken (by Lodovico, a faceless, purely representative character) from within Othello's rather than Iago's world: 'This heavy act with heavy heart *relate*.'

56

12.   It has frequently been noticed that Iago, like the Duke in *Measure for Measure* and Prospero, is a kind of playwright or director — it is he who moves the plot forward and licks it into shape. In fact his soliloquies could frequently be taken for the dramatist's own musings as he ponders the direction in which his play is going to go:

> Cassio's a proper man. Let me see now:
> To get his place, and to plume my will
> In double knavery. How? How? Let's see...

To Roderigo he explains:

> Thou knows't we work by wit, and not by witchcraft;
> And wit depends on dilatory time.

As the plot thickens he rehearses his moves to himself:

> Two things are to be done:
> My wife must move for Cassio to her mistress;
> I'll set her on;
> Myself the while to draw the Moor apart
> And bring him jump when he may Cassio find
> Soliciting his wife. Ay, that's the way!
> Dull not device by coldness and delay.

What this suggests is that if, in one sense, Othello triumphs in the end, in another it is Iago who triumphs. Not just because both Othello and Desdemona are dead, but because the making of the play *Othello* shows the triumph of plotting over story-telling. It is no accident that the play is so suited to grand opera (for, despite Frye's generalisations, opera too has its history), with its villain, early love duet, pathetic song for the heroine shortly before the end, mislaid handkerchiefs and final, long-drawn-out deaths. Of course, as I suggested in discussing Iago's drinking-song, the play escapes the limitations of Verdian opera in all kinds of ways; but the fact remains that Shakespeare, behind the scenes, is acting out a role which is closer to that of Iago than to that of Othello.

And how could this not be so? His audience is not 'the community'. It has paid to be entertained. Shakespeare has to make sure he keeps up their interest in a story which does not concern them directly. As Iago says, 'there are many events in the womb of time,' and it is the playwright's job, no less than Iago's desire, that 'they will be delivered'. Iago merely helps this along. It is *Shakespeare* who has Cassio leave just as Othello enters, who has Desdemona drop her handkerchief and Emilia pick it up and give it to Iago, who has her keep silent until it is too late. In *Othello* we watch Shakespeare exploring, in fascinated horror, the precise implications of his chosen vocation. From then on we will find him twisting and turning to escape Iago's logic, the logic which says that to deliver the events in the womb of time the dramatist must work secretly behind the scenes, manipulating his puppets in the interests of his plot.

13.   This is particularly noticeable in *Lear* and in *Antony and Cleopatra*. The central scenes in *Lear* are like an attempt to prolong the moment of Othello's fit, an attempt to escape from every constraint, social and linguistic and to return to the babelic origins of speech. But for Lear and for the playwright there is no escape and in the end plot re-asserts itself. In the light of what I have said so far this can only be seen as a deeply ambiguous triumph. In *Antony and Cleopatra*, however, a decisive step has been taken. Here there is no longer any fixed viewpoint. Each statement, each scene, is undercut by another. At the climax, as if challenging us to compare it with the end of *Othello*, Shakespeare makes the double death not out of the terrible pressure of tragic inevitability, but out of hundreds of tiny contradictory elements, so that even here we have no sense of unity. That is why it is a play which has given rise to more heated argument than any other, and why, perhaps, it

rarely succeeds in working in the theatre. It goes too much against those instincts which bring us to the theatre in the first place.

14. As if aware of this, Shakespeare, in his last plays, changed tack completely. He seems in those plays determined to throw overboard all that the Elizabethan theatre had gained, all that he himself had achieved in terms of psychological motivation and the organisation of plot. In *Hamlet* the dumb show had a clear dramatic function; in *Othello*, as I have tried to show, a kind of dumb show was the pivot of the action. In *Pericles* the dumb show is deliberately antitheatrical. The aged Gower, with his stumbling verses, makes no attempt to bring the audience into the action; on the contrary, he keeps us away from it. And the action itself, far from forming a plot that moves towards a climax, meanders through time, allowing us to respond to parallels and contrasts between episodes far apart in time, rather as the audience responded to *figura* in the miracle plays, never allowing us to enter the minds or feelings of the protagonists, but only to wonder at the patterns made by their actions.

Like Shakespeare's first comedy, *The Comedy of Errors*, *Pericles* is set in the traditionally magical island of Ephesus. But *Pericles* is everything *The Comedy of Errors* is not. Where that was all highly formalised New Comedy plot, identical twins and mistaken identities, this is all spectacle, story. It is as though Shakespeare, having, in *Hamlet* and *Lear*, tried to answer the questions: Who am I? What is man? — had recognised that such questions could never be answered within the work of art, and had decided not to conceal himself but to come out in front, as story-teller, between audience and play. Hamlet too, as has been remarked, acts in a sense as a mediator between the audience and a revenge tragedy. But Gower is no longer tormented by the implications of such a role: he serenely accepts it, stumbling forward on his clumsy lines:

59

To sing a song that old was sung,
From ashes ancient Gower is come...

15. *The Winter's Tale* adds the final element. It is fitting that
its analogue should be not an early comedy but *Othello* itself.
The other characters in the play, instead of being broken by
Leontes' jealousy, stand resolutely up to him, insisting that he
is living in a private world conjured up by his own imagination.
Hermione, accused, replies firmly:

> You speak a language that I understand not:
> My life stands in the level of your dreams,
> Which I'll lay down.

But though Leontes is quick to reply: 'Your actions are my
dreams', it is she who is right, and Leontes' jealous dreams
cannot stand up against the pressure of events. The death of
Mamilius, coming on top of Leontes' rejection of the oracle,
forces the whole edifice to crumble and he recovers his sanity as
quickly as he had lost it.

Leontes is the type of the tyrant, as Paulina keeps insisting,
the mad king who uses his power to try and force the world to
conform to his vision of it. But however powerful one is, one has
ultimately to yield to the reality of the world. When the gaoler
hesitates about letting Paulina leave with Hermione's new-
born baby, she answers:

> You need not fear it, sir:
> This child was prisoner to the womb, and is
> By law and process of great nature, thence
> Free'd and enfranchis'd; not a party to
> The anger of the king, nor guilty of
> (If any be) the trespass of the queen.

The child is prisoner in the womb, but not in the same way as
the mother is prisoner in Leontes' jail. It is the subject of the
law and process of great nature, not of any earthly king. But

how can great nature herself be contained within the imprisoning confines of a play?

In these last plays of his, Shakespeare is careful to show us that the plots turn on chance, not manipulation or psychology. It is Autolycus, selfish, cunning, innocent Autolycus, just as much as Perdita, who is the presiding spirit here, as we move into those extraordinary last acts, with their constant reminder that what we are seeing is stranger even than an old story, no better than a tuppenny ballad. Strange but true, and true because there it is, happening in front of our eyes.

But doesn't all drama take place in front of our eyes? Well .... Contrast, for example, the way Paulina sets up the last scene with the way Rosalind does so in *As You Like It*. In that play the audience knows what Rosalind but no one else knows. It is privy to all the secrets of the plot. The pleasure here, as in *Twelfth Night*, derives from seeing the characters gradually discover 'the truth', which we have known all the time. In *The Winter's Tale* Shakespeare gets rid of this aspect of the plot in a little scene where minor characters simply report and discuss the re-uniting of father and daughter. The climax is reserved for something else. Here we just sit and look. We are told our faith is required, and we give it, and watch a dead queen being conjured back to life with the help of music. This is of course what happened in Marlowe's *Doctor Faustus*. But where Helen was a spirit and Faustus and the audience doomed to be merely titillated by her, the effect of Hermione's appearance is entirely different. Like Gower, she personifies, embodies Time, and her presence before us is a gage of the bountifulness of time. In a miraculous moment Shakespeare reverses all romance conventions even as he brings them to a head: Leontes can take pleasure in his restored wife just *because* time has wrinkled her face; a Hermione unchanged in sixteen years would be a painted Hermione; that she has aged is a sign that she lives.

But there is more. This scene, in a sense, is the answer to

Othello, and it is important to see how. In the tragedy, I suggested, Iago stands between us and a kind of dumb show, and directs us as to how we are to interpret it. We watch someone leave and are immediately made to ask ourselves: Did he look furtive? Was he guilty? To make sense of the dramatic fiction we must all become Iagos. But in these last plays Shakespeare creates a kind of drama in which the Iago within us is accepted — and dismissed. It is not a plot that breeds in the womb of time, it is human life. We have seen Hermione before. Now we see her again. We watch with awe and wonder as she performs what is after all the simplest of stage actions: she steps forward. It does not *mean* anything; the wonder lies in the fact *that it is happening*.

It is nothing: a woman walking forward. And it is everything.

16.   Nevertheless, even here, plot re-asserts itself. Hermione opens her mouth and speaks:

> You gods, look down,
> And from your sacred vials pour your graces
> Upon my daughter's head!

She asks questions; she promises explanations. And though there is still one more wonder in store for both characters and audience, the play ends with Leontes asking Paulina to

> Lead us from hence, where we may leisurely
> Each one demand and answer to his part
> Performed in this wide gap of time since first
> We were dissevered. Hastily lead away.

The fact is that Shakespeare, in spite of everything, is at ease within the rhetorical tradition. He achieves such mastery that he can bend it to suit his will, but he would not dream of destroying it or rejecting it. He seems to sense and accept the fact that he can only have everything if he has nothing.

Yet Borges' story will not leave off haunting us. Is that

because we are not and cannot be the heirs of Shakespeare, but of Romanticism?

> Before a week was out he had returned to the village of his birth, where he recovered the trees and the river of his childhood, and he did not bind them to those others his muse had celebrated, those made illustrious by mythological allusions and Latin phrases.

According to Borges, Shakespeare, returning to Stratford determined to be *someone*, became a retired impresario and local businessman. But he could equally well have become a novelist. For the novel explicitly dissociates itself from mythological allusion and Latin phrases. It celebrates the trees and rivers of childhood; not that which has always been sung, but that which has never been sung before and which would have remained unsung had it not been for one person. The novel turns its back on convention and tradition and speaks about the world of each of us in our mother tongue. It is the free speech of free men.

But how free is free?

III

'Non Ego sed Democritus dixit'

————→•◆•◆•◆•←————

1.   'O word, thou word that I lack!' With that despairing cry
Schoenberg's only opera, *Moses und Aron*, breaks off at the end
of the second act. The music for the third was never composed.

We are, of course, dealing with a general issue, not one
particular to Schoenberg. Here, for example, is Henry James
in his *Notebooks*:

> The upshot of all such reflections is that I have only to let
> myself *go*! So I have said to myself all my life — so I said to
> myself in the far-off days of my fermenting and passionate
> youth. Yet I have never fully done it. The sense of it — of
> the need of it — rolls over me at times with commanding
> force: it seems the formula of my salvation, of what
> remains to me of a future.

Here is Lily Briscoe in *To the Lighthouse*:

> And she wanted to say not one thing, but everything.
> Little words that broke up the thought and dismembered
> it said nothing. 'About life, about death; about Mrs
> Ramsay' — no, she thought, one could say nothing to
> nobody. The urgency of the moment always missed its
> mark. Words fluttered sideways and struck the object
> inches too low. Then one gave up; then the idea sunk back
> again.... For how could one express in words these
> emotions of the body?

And here, finally, is Marcel in *A la recherche*:

> Because I wanted one day to be a writer, it was time to

decide what it was I intended to write. But as soon as I asked myself that question, seeking to find a subject of infinite philosophical significance, my mind stopped functioning, my attention seemed to focus only on emptiness, I felt that I had no genius, or that perhaps a cerebral disease prevented it from coming to birth.

Why this sense of the lack of a word that would make all the difference? Why this feeling that words are incapable of expressing the emotions of the body? Why this desire to write and the simultaneous sense that the desire has only to surface to be frustrated?

These are not questions that would have troubled Shakespeare or Mozart. I suggested last week that Shakespeare's famous patience, his ability to return all our questions, is perhaps rather less bland than critical discourse often makes it appear. But any doubts he might have are absorbed in a passionately joyful refusal to come to rest in any one position. And similarly Mozart, when, for example, he gives Figaro the wonderful aria 'Non piu andrai' which ends Act I of *The Marriage of Figaro* — Mozart is happy to enter the world of martial music and plunder it of its riches, bring it to life — in ironic counterpoint of course to the action — and then move on to something else.

Such easy commerce with the tradition seems no longer possible for the writers from whom I have just quoted. Why?

2.   Let's start with one of the great fictional attempts to confront the question head-on, Thomas Mann's *Doctor Faustus*.

No reader can fail to be struck, right from the start, by the way the book moves between garrulousness and silence. The garrulousness is the narrator's, Serenus Zeitblom, latter-day Humanist and teacher; the silence is Adrian Leverkühn's, the tragic composer who is the subject of the fictional biography. On the rare occasions when Adrian does write or speak, it is nearly always in the form of parody, as though he could only give utterance in the style and voice of someone else. And, on the few occasions when he seems to speak in his own voice, we get a strong sense of the pain every word causes him, and his brief remarks are usually punctuated with a laugh, as if to dismiss as pointless and redundant whatever he has just said.

An early clue to his attitude is provided by the scene in which Adrian's father is showing the boys some of the wonders of nature. These include a beautiful shell, covered with strange markings, reminiscent of Oriental calligraphy. But though people have tried to decipher them, they have been unsuccessful. 'It has turned out to be impossible,' says old Jonathan Leverkühn, 'to get at the meaning of these marks.... They refuse themselves to our understanding, and will, painfully enough, continue to do so.' And yet, he says, the very fact that the marks are there suggests 'that Nature painted these ciphers, to which we lack the key.' Something, then, is communicated here, but it is and will remain 'an inaccessible communication.' And Zeitblom comments: 'Even as a boy I clearly understood that Nature, outside of the human race, is fundamentally illiterate — that in my eyes is precisely what makes her uncanny.'

Adrian, on the other hand, finds this fascinating. Not just because he is more curious than his friend, but because he has less faith than him in the blessings of human literacy. Where Zeitblom is content to teach the classics, play the viola and respond to the beauty of works of art, Adrian is tormented by a doubt:

> The work of art? It is a fraud. It is something the burgher wishes there still were. It is contrary to truth, contrary to serious art. Genuine and serious is only the very short, the highly consistent musical moment.

Why a fraud? What has the 'burgher' to do with it? And what is Adrian implying when he remarks, immediately afterwards, that art would like 'to stop being only pretence and play'?

66

Zeitblom, paraphrasing Adrian's first and only teacher, Wendell Kretschmar, struggles to explain:

> In a work there is much seeming and sham, one could go further and say that as 'a work' it is seeming in and for itself. Its ambition is to make one believe that it is not made, but born, like Pallas Athene in full fig and embossed armour from Jupiter's head. But that is a delusion. Never did a work come like that. It is work: art-work for appearance's sake — and now the question is whether at the present stage of our consciousness, our knowledge, our sense of the truth, this little game is still permissible, still intellectually possible...., whether all seeming, even the most beautiful, even precisely the most beautiful, has not today become a lie.

The work of art appears to be like the shell, but its marks are made by man and not by nature. And, being made by man, it must be prepared to face the question: Why? Is there any justification for it? In the first lecture I referred to Lévi-Strauss's point that there is a biological link between horse and horse, but that the only link between two axes lies in the fact that both belong to the same system of representation. The question Adrian is raising is whether we have any uses for axes in our society today, and, if not, why they still go on being made. Is there any justification for axes, no matter how beautiful, if there is no wood to cut and there are more efficient means of dealing with one's enemies?

This is the Devil's point too in the central chapter of the book. The time for masterpieces is over, he claims. Today we are too full of doubts to write in the overpowering and uninhibited fashion of a Beethoven. Adrian tries to counter this. Surely, he says, there is always 'the possibility of spontaneous harmony between a man's own needs and the moment, the possibility of "rightness", of a natural harmony out of which one might create without a thought or any compulsion.' But he doesn't really believe this himself, and the Devil is really speaking for him (that, after all, is the source of his strength), when he answers: 'My dear fellow, the situation is too critical to be dealt with without critique.' And in case Adrian should be tempted to think that this was purely the result of social or political factors, which might change in time, he warns him that 'the prohibitive difficulties of the work lie deep in the work itself.... It no longer tolerates pretence and play, the fiction, the self-glorification of form.' Quite simply

> certain things are no longer possible. The pretence of feeling as a compositional work of art, the self-satisfied pretence of music itself, has become impossible, and no longer to be preserved — I mean the personal notion that prescribed and formalized elements shall be introduced as though they were the inviolable necessity of the single case.... My friend, it cannot go on ... the pretence of the bourgeois work of art.... It is all up with the once bindingly valid conventions, which guaranteed freedom of play.

For what is freedom? It is only 'another word for subjectivity, and some fine day ... she despairs of the possibility of being creative out of herself.'

The view of artistic history here presented by Mann may be oversimplified, but it is profoundly suggestive (much more so than the purely linear views put forward in most histories of art: Augustans followed by Romantics followed by Victorians, etc.). Once, Mann argues, there was an art which was linked to the cult and subservient to it (axes were necessary because they were needed). Then, with the collapse of the cult in the Renaissance and Reformation, there emerged an art based on subjectivity, the art we associate with Michaelangelo and Beethoven. Beethoven took hold of the sonata form, which had until then been made up of roughly equal parts, each with its precise rhetorical function, and so filled out the development section that the form itself was altered beyond recognition. But the only rules for the making of this new kind of work were the desires and creative imagination of the artist, and, once men had lost Beethoven's confidence in his own will, what was there to put in its place? The situation Leverkühn inherits is that of being Beethoven's heir without the latter's optimistic belief in himself or the world. Beethoven shattered the playfulness of the more purely rhetorical forms of the eighteenth century, but what he has put in its place is no longer viable. How then is art any longer possible for the artist who takes his calling seriously and is not content simply to pander to the tastes of the public?

3.   Mann's analysis is of course meant to reflect on more than music. We can easily replace 'sonata form' by, say, Shakespearian comedy, or Beethoven by Victor Hugo. For Mann himself, though, this was his most sustained exploration of the value and meaning of the art in pursuit of which he had spent the greater part of his life — the art of the novelist.

We use the words *novel* and *roman* without giving them a thought. But those words may tell us more about the form than many a scholarly disquisition. In the Middle Ages Latin was the common language of Europe. It is difficult for us to realise the immense importance of this fact for men of the time. A recent historian gives us a glimpse of this when he writes:

> All who do not speak Latin are barbarians, don't really speak, don't have a language, merely utter cries like animals. The writers, even those who write in the vulgar tongue, imbued with a respect for 'clergie', make of Latin a synonym for language itself. In William IX of Aquitaine, as in Chretien de Troyes, the birds sing 'in their Latin' ('en leur latin').

Opposed to Latin is *roman*, the romance language, the vernacular. The term soon came to apply to a literary form, but it was a long time before it lost its old meaning.

The intrusion of the vernacular tongue into the empire of *latinitas* created a crisis of which Mann's book is only one of the more recent manifestations. It is interesting in this context to recall Dante's concern to explain (to himself and to his fellow writers) why it was that he should attempt an epic to rival Virgil's not in Latin but in the vernacular, and to recall too that only fifty years after the completion of the *Commedia* Petrarch was to take the decision to write *his* epic in Latin. What Marthe Robert has called the perpetual struggle of the old and the new, which Dante, uniquely, managed to resolve, has, with Petrarch, resulted in the triumph of the old, of Authority, over the new, the vernacular, Experience.

But it was of course Experience, in the guise of the novel, which was to have the last laugh. For, as Roger Dragonetti has pointed out:

> If the word *roman* has maintained itself through so many centuries, despite its own semantic contestations, as the term which designates a genre in perpetual renewal, this is no doubt because the revolutionary, transformational element, and especially the idea of a new language of literature, implied by the word *roman*, was more important than the content of the work.

The application of these remarks to the term *novel* hardly needs underlining. In England the drama seems to have succeeded the epic as the central form in the 1590s, and to have in turn been ousted by the novel in the 1740s. Scholars have often noted the links between the rise of the novel and the social and intellectual changes of the seventeenth century. More important, perhaps, is to realise that both *roman* and *novel* imply not another genre, but an escape from all genre, from the authority of culture enshrined in the notions of *Latin* and of *art*. The novel is the free utterance of free men.

But, as I asked at the end of the last lecture, how free is free?

4. Let us stay with this conflict between Latin and the vernacular for a moment. And let us return to Dante.

When Dante and Virgil at last leave the tenfold circlings of the penultimate pit of Hell, they find themselves in an eerie darkness, 'less than night and less than day'. Out of this darkness there emerges a dolorous sound, louder than thunder, more terrible than the sound Roland blew when Charlemagne's host was routed by the infidel. In the murky light Dante makes out an array of huge towers, but Virgil explains that these are giants, whose feet stand in the lower circle and whose upper bodies only are visible. As they approach the first of these figures the enormous mouth opens and meaningless sounds come forth: 'Raphel may amecche zabi almi.' Virgil explains to Dante:

> He is his own accuser: this is Nimrod, through whose ill thought one language only is not used in the world. Let us leave him alone and not speak in vain, for every language is to him as his is to others, which is known to none.

But Nimrod (the instigator of Babel, according to Midrashic tradition here followed by Dante) is only an extreme example of a tendency present in the *Inferno* right from the start. His sin, like that of all the damned, is essentially that of pride, placing himself before all others, and it is not surprising that this has infected his speech. For, wanting to utter that which is uniquely his, he cuts himself off from language altogether.

It seems as if our contrast of Latin and the vernacular was not as clear-cut as we had supposed. For if Latin is the language of *others*, of Authority, of the dominant culture, it does not follow that the vernacular is the opposite of these things. To use language at all is to use an instrument which is forged by others. It is not that the purely personal cannot be uttered in Latin; it cannot be uttered in language at all. Nimrod, thinking that it can — or thinking perhaps that he is speaking the language of Jonathan Leverkühn's shell, the

71

language of nature itself — is reduced to merely uttering noises.

What then is the writer to do who, for whatever reason, has turned his back on Latin and on the whole public world of rhetoric and mythology? The question did not worry many writers before this century, but it did worry Sterne, for he placed as an epigraph to Volumes V and VI of *Tristram Shandy* a quotation, *in Latin*, from Erasmus: '*Non ego sed Democritus dixit.*' Not I but Democritus said it. And to add to the point, Sterne did not get this straight from Erasmus but via Burton's *Anatomy of Melancholy*. As it stands the epigraph is a mock excuse for any material which might offend in what follows. But it is surely more than that. Like Chaucer's similar disclaimer at the start of *The Canterbury Tales*, it is an ironic reminder to the reader who thinks he is going to read the very words of Tristram or of Sterne (for after all the book is entitled *The Life and Opinions of Tristram Shandy*), that of course he will be doing nothing of the sort. For all languages are foreign languages — foreign to us, that is to say. *I* don't say it, Democritus (or whoever) does; it is never *my* language, for 'I' have no language.

Kafka put it rather more tragically when he wrote in his diary for 19 January 1922: 'What meaning have yesterday's conclusions today? They have the same meaning as yesterday, are true, except that the blood is oozing away in the chinks between the great stones of the law.'

Words are like the stones of the law. They are what can and must be said. But the blood of the individual oozes like the minutes and seconds of his life — *his* life, the only one he has — between the stones, the words, and there is no way of turning the hardness of stone into the fluidity of blood, or of congealing blood into stone.

5.   Barthes, in S/Z, has demonstrated with ruthless elegance the degree to which the language of the classical novel is made

up of modes of discourse speaking through the writer rather than for him. I have no wish to go once again over ground he has explored so thoroughly. But perhaps the very elegance of his analysis and the hardly concealed ferocity of his onslaught on Balzac have made us focus on certain aspects of the situation at the expense of others. At any rate, I would like to approach the problem from a slightly different angle. I want to focus not so much on the kinds of languages that get into novels as on the much bigger, more dangerous and intractable question of the writer's own sense of freedom and constraint.

I want to suggest that we should take the *dixit* in Sterne's epigraph in the widest possible sense. *Non ego sed Democritus dixit* suggests that where we thought we were free to make our destinies as individuals or as a group, we are in fact *being spoken*, or *being written*, by forces outside us. We are not speakers so much as parrots. Of course these forces do not constitute some transcendent being or historical necessity, but rather the multiplicity of conflicting and ever-changing pressures which make up what we take to be 'reality'. But the point is that the medieval optimism in history and the world as examples of God's discourse have here been ironically inverted, and the medieval notion of man as superior to the animals because capable of speech becomes God's last bad joke on us.

Let me remind you of two classic and influential nineteenth-century statements of this view. Marx's *Eighteenth Brumaire of Louis Bonaparte* opens with the famous remark: 'Hegel says somewhere that all the great events and characters of world history occur, so to speak, twice. He forgot to add: the first time as tragedy, the second as farce.' This, suggests Marx, has happened in France, with Louis Blanc in the role of Robespierre and Louis Napoleon in that of his famous uncle. Marx goes on:

Men make their own history, but not of their own free will: not under circumstances they themselves have chosen but under the given and inherited circumstances with which they are directly confronted. The traditions of dead generations weigh like a nightmare on the minds of the living.

(Years later Eliot was to make the same point about literary tradition:

> If our predecessors cannot teach us to write better than themselves they will surely teach us to write worse; because we have never learnt to criticise Keats, Shelley and Wordsworth (poets of assured though modest merit), Keats, Shelley and Wordsworth punish us from their graves with the annual scourge of the Georgian anthology.)

My second example comes from Freud. Freud's first work in psychoanalysis, the *Studies on Hysteria*, which he wrote with Breuer, contains the seeds of many of his later works. What he demonstrates here is that the patients who came to Breuer and himself suffering from hysterical paralysis were in fact acting out a personal drama *on their own bodies*. What their minds denied, their bodies affirmed. Yet part of them wished to understand what it was their bodies were concealing from them. Freud thus had to 'read' the hieroglyphics of their bodies in order to understand what they were really trying to tell him. But he could not do this on his own. He needed their collaboration. This was the origin of what one of the patients herself was to call 'the talking cure'. By talking, not necessarily telling the truth, but simply talking *to* someone, they were eventually able to give Freud enough information to allow him to reconcile their minds with their bodies and so cure them. Or so he optimistically thought at the time.

In these patients of Freud's we can see a kind of ironic echo of the Symbolist ideal of the speaking body — Yeats's admiration for Donne's line, 'one might almost say her body thought' is only the most famous example. One way of describing the relation between the two might be to say that it is rather like that between the two Napoleons. And in both the historical and the personal drama we can see a reflection of Sterne's epigraph: *Non ego sed Democritus dixit*. For it is not really *I* who speak, so much as those other, impersonal forces, forces which can perhaps best be designated by the impersonal language of Latin.

6.   Freud and Marx are confident that they can tame those forces, that *their* language can encompass them, reduce them to intelligibility. The artists are less sure. 'Her painful legs' said Freud about a patient, 'began to "join in the conversation" during our analysis.' In Kafka and early Eliot too arms and legs seem to 'join in the conversation', though what exactly the conversation is about they do not know.

I don't have to remind you how meticulously Kafka describes the gestures people make. He has to be precise because these gestures always seem to be on the point of revealing something decisive about the person making them, though of course in the end they never do. And when seen from the point of view of the gesticulator they suggest a kind of anxiety, as though by the jerkiness of his movements he would find his way back to his natural environment. In a diary entry for 1922 he actually compares the gestures of the body to writing:

> Strange how make-believe, if engaged in systematically enough, can change into reality. Childish games (though I was well aware that they were so) marked the beginning of my intellectual decline. I deliberately cultivated a facial tick, for instance, or would walk across the Graben with arms crossed behind my head. A repulsive, childish... game. (My writing began in the same way; only later on its development came to a halt, unfortunately.)

This passage suggests what many of the letters, diary entries, and of course those line drawings scattered through his diaries,

75

all confirm: that Kafka is as though embarrassed by the number of possibilities open to him at every second of the day; not just all the possible ways of writing any one sentence, but all the possible ways of moving, nodding, waving.... If there is no natural way to exist — or if I for some reason or other have never been initiated into it — then is not the very basis of my existence suspect?

The early poetry of Eliot too is full of people who try to keep going by imitating the words and gestures of those around them, since they seem unable to act instinctively. Prufrock, forever climbing the stairs to where women move purposefully and talk confidently about Michaelangelo, is only the most famous of these:

> And indeed there will be time
> To wonder 'Do I dare?' and, 'Do I dare?'
> Time to turn back and descend the stair,
> With a bald spot in the middle of my hair —
> (They will say: 'How his hair is growing thin!')
> My morning coat, my collar mounting firmly to the chin,
> My necktie rich and modest, but asserted by a simple pin —
> (They will say: 'But how his arms and legs are thin!')

He is a sentient void on which articles of clothing have been hung, his very language that of the fashion magazines ('My necktie rich and modest, but *asserted* by a simple pin...'). He seems to talk about nothing but himself, yet that 'self' is made up of clothes he hardly seems to have chosen, and of words which are as external to himself as the clothes.

There are many like Prufrock in early Eliot. Chief among them is perhaps Mr Eliot himself:

> How unpleasant to meet Mr. Eliot!
> With his features of clerical cut,
> And his brow so grim
> And his mouth so prim

76

And his conversation so nicely
Restricted to What Precisely
And If and Perhaps and But.
With a bobtail cur
In a coat of fur
And a porpentine cat
And a wopsical hat:
How unpleasant to meet Mr. Eliot!
        (Whether his mouth be open or shut).

7. And yet, if the gestures of Kafka and Eliot are no more a
'true' expression of their 'true' selves than those of Louis
Napoleon or Freud's patients, there is a difference. What we
have here, after all, are not gestures, but poems, stories. And
we read them as such, as the 'description of a struggle', to use
the title of one of Kafka's earliest stories, rather than as the
struggle itself.

The Chinese spy in 'The Garden of Forking Paths' thinks he
is a free agent, influencing the course of history, but he is only
playing his allotted role in the labyrinth which is what history
really is. Borges's Shakespeare escapes from the meaningless
proliferation of rhetorical exercises in the dramatic mode by
retiring to Stratford and becoming a local business man. The
hero of 'Tlön, Uqbar, Orbis Tertius' reacts to the takeover of
the world by a purely idealistic universe by retreating to a
lonely hotel and working on his 'uncertain Quevedian translation...of Browne's *Urn Burial*.' His Symbolist poet, Pierre
Menard, takes a more aggressive attitude. Sterne had only
placed his quotation from Erasmus as an epigraph. Pierre
Menard devotes his life to rewriting *Don Quixote*. Not in the
vulgar sense of Joyce rewriting *The Odyssey* or Anouilh rewriting Greek tragedy, but in a pure mad symbolist way:

> He did not want to compose another *Quixote* — which is
> easy — but *the Quixote*. It is unnecessary to add that he
> never envisaged a mechanical transcription of the original:

he didn't propose to copy it. His admirable intention was to reproduce a few pages which would coincide word for word and line for line with those of Miguel de Cervantes.

Unlike, say, the poems of Mallarmé, *Don Quixote* is full of contingent, haphazard details. To write it again would therefore entail discovering and somehow tapping not merely the inner logic of a work of art, but the very language of nature. To write *Don Quixote* — or any novel — is easy, and, in a sense, pointless. It only requires the ability to deaden one's critical instinct and a capacity for hard, unrewarding work. But to *rewrite* it would mean escaping at last from the unknown forces speaking through one, being truly master of one's destiny.

8.   Only by resolutely refusing to speak in his own voice does Pierre Menard find his voice. I have already said that Adrian Leverkühn adopts a somewhat similar solution. His silence, as I said, strikes the reader from the start. And even when he does speak or write letters, he employs a curious kind of mock sixteenth-century diction and style, as if to deny what he is saying in the very act of saying it. Zeitblom senses what is going on when, talking of a letter of Adrian's, he says that 'its style was of course intended as a parody of the grotesque Halle experiences and the language idiosyncrasies of Ehrenfried Kumpf. At the same time it both hides and reveals his own personality and stylistic leanings.' In fact, he suggests, what Leverkühn is doing is using 'quotation as disguise', 'parody as pretext.'

Parody and quotation are bound to upset the Humanist Zeitblom, for they suggest an easy alliance between self and expression, art and culture. They also clearly troubled Thomas Mann. Yet what is his own novel? Looked at in one way it seems to be an old-fashioned fictional biography, written in a straightforward linear way. But this is Zeitblom's work, not Mann's. And to Zeitblom's surprise elements keep creeping into the books which are anything but linear. Looked at at little more closely, in fact, the book seems to be constructed more on serialist than on classical lines. Not only that. It is also a huge collage of quotation, historical material, *objets trouvés*, placed next to each other, with no connecting links. If at first sight it seems to be written by Zeitblom, in the end we are left wondering if it is not perhaps Leverkühn's last, parodistic testament, merely usurping the tones and sentiments of Zeitblom as pretext and disguise.

I said last week that there would appear to be a kind of safety in parody. But perhaps we should distinguish between two kinds of parody. There is the type exemplified by Shakespeare's parody of inkhorn and bombast, which is conducted from a position of superiority, so to speak, and there is parody which is in effect collage. It can be as extreme and desperate as it is in Leverkühn's compositions or in the music-theatre works of Peter Maxwell Davies, or it can be as cool and ironic as it is in Stravinsky's neo-classical compositions. The important thing is that what we have here is an aesthetic of *making* rather than one of *expression*. The mouth is gagged but the hands are free.

9.   Let me give you some examples of such an aesthetic in action.

Consider, for instance, what Eliot is able to say by the most obvious kind of making: cutting a quotation out of its place in a continuum and placing it in a new context. I won't go into any of the complex examples in *The Waste Land*, but will confine myself to something much simpler, to epigraphs. As you will see, that is already quite complicated enough.

The two epigraphs I have chosen are both taken from Dante, and they form ten of the first twelve lines which any reader of Eliot's *Collected Poems* will encounter. I will take the second one first. It is the epigraph to 'The Love Song of J. Alfred Prufrock', and appears, in italics, just below the title:

79

S'io credesse che mia risposta fosse
A persona che mai tornasse al mondo,
Questa fiamma staria senza piu scosse.
Ma perciocche giammai di questo fondo
Non torno vivo alcun, si'i'odo il vero,
Senza tema d'infamia ti rispondo.

Eliot's work, like that of many modern artists, has been accused of being unreal, unlocated in time or place. Nothing could be further from the truth. But its time is *now* and its place *here*. We are involved in a completely new conception of time. In most literature the words make their own sensual impact, but they also send us back and away into a unified world of time. In Eliot the gap between title and epigraph, between epigraph and first line ('Let us go then you and I') becomes something palpable, something we have to cross and something we feel ourselves crossing. The reader of early Eliot is like a steeplechaser: now a high hurdle, now a water jump, now a seductive stretch of flat. Our natural critical — self-preservative? — instinct is to remove the obstacles. This is a mistake; for the obstacles *are* the poem.

To return to the quotation. As Hugh Kenner has said, the most important thing about these epigraphs is that they ease us into the poem so that we never know how or where or even if the poem has begun. The title speaks of a love song, but the epigraph is propelled forward by a dry crabbed logic very far removed from either love or song: 'If I thought the person I was addressing would be returning to the world above I wouldn't speak openly, as I'm now doing; but, knowing he won't, I will . . .'. Is the speaker then Prufrock, and is it us he is addressing, as he is to do in the opening lines of the poem? Or is it someone talking *to* Prufrock? In Dante the lines are spoken by the wily councellor Guido to Dante himself, who will of course return to the world above, and, what's more, will write down everything Guido says for all posterity to read. So: is the speaker still Guido? And if so are we Dante? Or is Prufrock Dante? Or is Prufrock Guido? Or are we both Prufrock and Guido? Or is the quote only tangentially related to the poem, giving it a particular *tone* and no more? How, in fact, *does* the epigraph relate to the poem?

To ask that is to throw into question the whole unity of the poem, of poems in general. For if we are uncertain about the relation of epigraph to poem, what of the relation of the first line of the poem proper to any of its subsequent lines?

We know the difficulty Eliot had in deciding what should go into *The Waste Land* and what should be left out. We know that Proust went on adding to the bulk of *A la recherche* until the day he died, and that at the end he had to admit to himself that what he was making was not, as he had hoped, a cathedral, but only a patchwork dress. Is not the notion of a work of art itself one of those ideas Leverkühn and the Devil felt could no longer be taken for granted? Who is to say where such a work will begin, where end, once you have discarded the rhetorical rules of form that guided a Milton, and have renounced their nineteenth-century substitutes, subjective passion and fictional plotting?

These questions hover over Eliot's poetry. The fact that generations of students have pored over the poems has somehow made it seem necessary that they mean *something*. But what if they don't mean anything? What if they exist only as an area of tension, not as repositories of meaning? Is not one's feeling on reading them more like glimpsing a snake glide through long grass? There is a stirring, then all is still. Like the magi, we have witnessed something, and that something was good, and we cannot find it again — except by rereading the poems.

The epigraph has alerted us to something in Eliot's poetry. But perhaps it is not unique to Eliot. Perhaps this is something which is true of all poetry; only in Eliot's case the poetry is stripped of the appearance of being something else.

Let me return to the other quotation. This one appears on the title page of the whole volume: *Prufrock and Other Observations*, 1917. Remember that we are dealing with the first book of poems by a little known American living in England. the title page bears a dedication: 'For Jean Verdenal, 1889-1915, mort aux Dardanelles.' then comes the quotation, in italics:

> la quantitate
> Puote veder del amor che a te mi scalda,
> Quando dismento nostra vanitate
> Trattando l'ombre come cosa salda.

Here the foreign language does not strike us as secretive so much as private. After all, a dedication is a kind of public private letter. We do not know Jean Verdenal, but clearly he was a friend of Eliot's who was killed in the Dardanelles campaign. We take this in and then almost avert our eyes from what follows, for this is even more than the usual dedication: it is a private message to someone who is dead. It has therefore all that much more authority and weight, since nothing that can now happen can make Eliot alter it.

What does it say? Roughly: 'You can see how much love I have for you when I treat the shadow as the real thing.' Verdenal is now dead, Eliot seems to be saying, but he is dedicating the book to him as to a living person, and this refusal to accept that he is dead shows how dearly he loves him. For Eliot, Verdenal will always be a living presence.

This time too we gain something, though by no means everything, from being familiar with the original and its context. Dante's poem is full of wonderful, joyful meetings: with his ancestor Cacciaguida in Heaven; with his old teacher, Brunetto Latini, in Hell; with his master Virgil at the outset. But no meeting is more full of mingled joy and sadness than the one between the two pilgrims and Statius on the upper slopes of Mt Purgatory. Statius, one of the last great poets of antiquity,

a Christian like Dante but a Roman poet like Virgil, does not
know who the two are who meet him, and he tells them about
himself:

> I sang of Thebes, and then of the great Achilles, but I fell
> on the way with my second burden. [He never finished his
> second epic.] The sparks which warmed me from the
> divine flame whereby more than a thousand have been
> kindled were the seeds of my poetic fire: I mean the *Aeneid*,
> which in poetry was both mother and nurse to me — with-
> out it I had achieved little of worth; and to have lived
> yonder when Virgil lived I would consent to one sun more
> than I owe to my coming forth from exile. (P.xxi. 92-102)

Virgil motions to Dante to keep silent, but Statius has already
caught the beginnings of a smile on his face, and asks Dante to
explain the reason. When he learns who it is he has been
speaking to,

> Already he was stooping to embrace my teacher's feet; but
> he said to him, 'Brother, do not so, for you are a shade and
> a shade you see.'
> And he, rising, 'Now you may comprehend the measure
> of the love that burns in me for you, when I forget our
> emptiness and treat shades as solid things.'

Statius's action and Virgil's reply is itself already a re-
enactment of an episode in the *Aeneid*. This is Dante's way of
paying extra, silent homage to Virgil. It is quite extraordinary
to me that these lines, written in another language than his
own, by another poet, spoken by a third about a fourth, should
come through at the start of Eliot's volume with such heart-
breaking directness: the only 'sincere' words, we could say, in
the entire volume.

10.   Let us turn from poetry to prose. We open a recent novel
by Muriel Spark, *Territorial Rights*, and read the following

sentence (Muriel Spark seems to me to be one of the few major living writers still producing work worthy of her best, so I make no apology for placing her beside Eliot. She can survive that.):

> The bureau clerk was telephoning to the Pensione Sofia while Robert Leaver watched the water-traffic at the ferry and the off-season visitors arriving in Venice.

This appears to do its work as efficiently as any one of a hundred fairly good novels. But, though we don't fully register it at the time, I think we stumble slightly over 'telephoning to' — 'the bureau clerk was telephoning to the Pensione Sofia . . .' We read on, nonetheless, and a few lines later come upon the sentence:

> It was his first visit to Venice and he was young: but he had only half a mind to feel enchanted, the other half being still occupied with a personal anxiety in Paris from where he had just come.

Now there can no longer be any doubt about it. 'Occupied with a personal anxiety in Paris' is not what the narrator would say, it is what Robert would say. In a way not uncommon for novels, the narrative remains in the third person but mimes the words or thoughts of the protagonist. What is disconcerting about this book is that there is no protagonist, no central character whose way of thinking might influence the narrative. Or rather, there is such a character, but he is dead, cut in half, and buried on either side of a well-kept Venetian garden.

The narrative drives along at a firm brisk pace, but we gradually come to see that its briskness is all too suspect. It seems to have no will of its own. Without seeming to be aware of it, it accepts into itself totally incompatible modes of discourse — 'as always, full of the Curran idea'; 'That afternoon she slipped out with the courage of her wild convictions and the dissatisfaction that has no name' — leaving us with the sense of something more round the corner, something which badly needs to be said, but which never is. I cannot think of another novel which gives us so strong a sense of what Wittgenstein meant when he said: 'I cannot use language to get outside language.'

The action, as I've said, hinges on a dead body, buried in the garden of the Pensione Sofia after being cut in two, so that each of the two sisters who had loved the murdered man may have her share of his remains. The body is never uncovered, but a great deal of money, a great many words, and some affection, are made to circulate as a result of its presence. 'There's the question of the body,' one of the characters delightfully remarks. 'The rest is immaterial.'

The point is beautifully made. It is the answer to the remarks of James and Schoenberg with which I began. For them there seemed to be a fullness of language, somewhere, waiting to be grasped. Yet it would always evade them. Spark suggests that there is indeed an underlying plenitude or truth, but it is not another language, better, more truthful, richer, than the one we possess. Rather, it is the ground of all languages, that without which they would not exist, but which none of them can conjure up. As the butcher says to Robert: 'You see, *figlio mio*, they have the body in the garden, sliced in two. That's concrete. Everything else is anything you like.' Not everything is anything you like, as some recent novelists have suggested, but *everything else*, apart from the buried, dismembered body.

11.   I will draw out the implications of these remarks in a moment. But first I want to present you with two more examples of what I have called an aesthetic of making as opposed to an aesthetic of expression, one from music and one from painting.

Like Eliot and Muriel Spark, Stravinsky 'found himself' very early on in his career. After a few years of competent but unexciting late Romantic music, he suddenly changed direction and began to work, like Eliot, with small fragments, constantly repeated and starkly juxtaposed. This was to be his way of working for the rest of his long rich musical life. As Alexander Goehr has recently pointed out, each such fragment 'is defined by an absolute duration; the manner of duration is "real" — by addition, rather than "psychological".' The work is built up by means of these blocks of pure time, giving Stravinsky's music that immediacy, that lack of a contrast between foreground and background, which we have already seen at work in Eliot.

But once the approach to musical creation is conceived in this way, as the making of something, not the expression of an emotion, then the consequences are far-reaching. Schoenberg, wedded to an expressionist aesthetic, is forced to abandon his only opera for lack of that 'Word' which would be its justification. Stravinsky, we could say, does not keep reaching out *beyond*; he re-examines what is in front of him: words, sounds, and their relation. Years later he was to say about *Renard*:

> I planned the staging myself, and always with the consideration that it should not be confounded with opera. The players are to be dancing acrobats and the singers are not to be identified with them: ... as in *Les Noces*, the performers, musical and mimetic, should all be together on the stage, with the singers in the centre of the musical ensemble.

Les Noces is the great work of the 1912-22 period, and Stravinsky's description of what he wanted to achieve there is very illuminating:

> *Les Noces* is a suite of typical wedding episodes told through quotations of typical talk. The latter, whether the bride's, the groom's, the parents' or the guests', is always

ritualistic. As a collection of clichés and quotations of typical wedding sayings, it might be compared to one of those scenes in *Ulysses* in which the reader seems to be over-hearing scraps of conversation without the connecting thread of discourse. But *Les Noces* might also be compared to *Ulysses* in the larger sense that both works are trying to *present* rather than to *describe*.

'Scraps of conversation without the connecting thread of discourse'; 'to present rather than to describe' — of course Stravinsky is talking a long time after the event, but he is accurately describing not only his own work in those years, but also that of his greatest contemporaries. The recent Picasso exhibitions, in Paris, New York and London, in which for the first time we were able to see many of the works in the artist's own collection, only served to reinforce the parallel between the painter and the composer. For what emerged so strongly from them was the paramount importance of *making* in all Picasso's art: our vision of the world is enhanced because something, no matter how small, has been made, *put together*. It is the *papiers collés* and the first made objects of the pre-war years, not the *Demoiselles d'Avignon*, we can now see, which were the heralds of the future. As with Stravinsky and Eliot, so here, one feels the excitement generated by the substitution of the notion of *pro*duction for that of *re*production. Quite rightly Daix and Rosselot, in their great catalogue of the Cubist years, point out that with the first *papiers collés*

painting is reduced to the signifier, its material support. Neither the thing signified by perspective, nor the organis-ing anecdote, nor a resemblance to objects or perspective intervenes in the way the spectator relates to the subject the artist submits to him. Here we have the final stages of the evolution initiated by Manet's pictorial silence: the elimination of the subject.

Yet, they go on to point out, 'this is not abstract painting. It is true that it can be read as abstract painting; but it maintains very obvious connections with the concrete. Only these connections are contradictory.'

Thus if we turn to the 'Table with Wineglass and Bottle of Bass', made in Paris early in 1914 (No. 656 in Daix and Rosselot), we can see that what Picasso is really doing is testing what is the minimum requirement for the viewer to be able to 'read' the work as existing in illusionist space. He draws the corner of a table in normal perspective, then, where we would expect to find the flattened parallelogram dictated by the traditional viewpoint, he places an irregularly cut square of paper which overlaps the square field left for it and forms a rough rectangular projection. This is just big enough to comprise the other corner of the table, drawn in quite a different manner from the first. On this piece of paper he places two shapes cut out of paper, a very large one for the glass and an absurdly small one for the bottle of Bass. This last is placed within a larger cutout, which reflects it like a sort of shadow. Finally, sawdust is stuck on the first two cutouts to give them a slight relief. The whole functions within a Cubist space which is both adjacent to and also within the perspective space of the table leg, which is drawn straight on to the cardboard support.

The point of all this is not, with Picasso, as it was with some of his contemporaries, mere decoration. It is part of his continued and passionate analysis of spatial syntax. Curiously, nothing succeeds in disturbing our re-creation of space — as with Sterne, we accept the most flagrant contradictions. And yet such constructions are curiously exhilarating to contemplate. They help us to rediscover the world because, depicting it other, they force us to recognise why it is as it is.

More perhaps than any of the other artists working at the time. Picasso was interested in the outside world. His question is always: How, by making something, can I discover more

Reproduced by courtesy of Editions Ides et Calendes, Neuchatel.

about the world? Making is always a step into the unknown. You start with that which is immediate, to hand, and suddenly you have left all safe ground. When Apollinaire said of him at the time that it was as if 'a new-born child were re-ordering the universe for his own personal use, and to facilitate his relationship with his fellow-men', he caught something of the excitement generated by Picasso's work, but he did not perhaps stress enough the way making, the work of the hand, contributed to discovery: for the re-ordering is perpetual, the world is remade with every canvas, every mark.

12.   It is easy to see the similarities that exist between the approaches of the artists I have been discussing: Borges, Mann, Eliot, Spark, Stravinsky, Picasso. If what I have said about them is correct then one way of describing what they are up to is to say that they have more in common with those Mann called the artists of the cult than with the artists of subjective individualism. The medieval poet was, after all, called a *maker*, and if we go back even further, to the epic poets of oral cultures, the similarities are even more striking. The epic poet put together his poem by means of blocks, the oral formulae, and he thought of himself not as having anything to express but rather as the voice and memory of the community.

But we have only to put it like this to be struck at once by the enormous differences. The oral poet makes a public object; his task is to create something, which will be common property, which will fall into the established patterns and bring to life again the established traditions. But the modern artist makes — what?

This is the question to which I have been leading in the course of this lecture. There is an answer to it which is persuasive, so persuasive, in fact, that it seems to have established itself as *the* answer, but which I believe to be profoundly misleading. Let me try and sum it up for you.

Once upon a time, it goes, there were artists and there were works of art. But today, because we have at last realised that a work of art is not natural, like a horse, but part of a system of representations, like an axe, we can see that this notion of an artist or author was a myth, perpetuated by a whole ideology of the subject. We know now that the artist is a maker. He puts his material together for the sheer pleasure of it, and any relation it may have with the real world is purely coincidental. A fortune-teller needs to know what the cards *mean*, says Robbe-Grillet, a bridge-player only how they are *used*. The artist is a player.

This is persuasive because it is of course partly true. And it is backed by the entire thrust of what has come to be called structuralist criticism. But I hope my earlier discussion of Sterne, and my analysis today of other examples will have made you feel uneasy with it. The very elegance and simplicity of this model should make us suspect it. A work of art, I suggested in my first lecture, is more like a man than like an axe; it partakes of the orders of both culture and nature. What I have been suggesting today is that the modern artist, recognising the impossibility of speaking in his own voice, is indeed a maker; but what is important about his work is not that he makes an object or plays a game, but the sense he conveys of the act of making itself.

You recall Frye's illuminating comment upon Shakespeare's impartiality:

> It is curious that we think of impartiality only as detachment, of devotion to craftsmanship only as purism, an attitude which, as in Flaubert, turns all human life into an enormously intricate still life, like the golden touch of Midas... Shakespeare's impartiality is a totally involved and committed impartiality: it expresses itself in bringing everything equally to life.

Now there is a view of art expressed by certain modern writers — Flaubert, Joyce, Nabokov, Robbe-Grillet, John Barth —

which sees the artist as standing above the fray, indifferent, Godlike, paring his fingernails. This attitude is often taken, by both supporters and opponents of modern art, to represent its essential position. I would like to suggest that this is a misleading view, and one which is frequently given the lie by the very works of the artists who uphold it.

I suggested last week that there is a profound link between Malvolio and Iago, that Malvolio's experience precipitated Iago, so to speak. Iago is the way the self instinctively protects itself when it finds itself alone in the dark, with voices telling it it is mad. Freud would have called it the superego. And if this Iago self can be seen at work in the complex plotting of the traditional novel, it can also be seen in the retreat to a narcissistic playfulness on the part of the writers I have just mentioned. As I say, this is not necessarily the dominant aspect of their work, but it is a definite temptation, and one to which they all at one time or another succumb. It is of course a temptation to which all artists who have faced Leverkühn's crisis are particularly prone. It would be natural for Eliot or Muriel Spark to give in to it, as it seems to me in his last works Nabokov gave in to it; to say: I cannot express the unique river of my childhood, so I will play with mythology and Latin allusions in order to show that I believe in none of it.

But what we have seen in Borges and Eliot and Spark is quite another attitude: a deep desire to express, along with a recognition that it is impossible to express. 'There is a goal but no way,' says Kafka. And what he means can I think be understood by recalling Sterne's nostalgia for a time when orators had something to hide under the cloaks, and Spark's wicked novel about a corpse which is the centre of the action. There is something there, but it can never be spoken, for it is not a hidden object but the ground of all speech. We cannot find it or say it, we can only embody it in action, the action of making, of reading.

I have already mentioned the narrator of Borges's story,

'Tlön, Uqbar, Orbis Tertius', who reacts to the gradual take-over of the real world by a parallel idealist universe by retiring to a provincial hotel and getting on with his translation of Thomas Browne's *Urn Burial*. There is nothing very grandiose about that, but the point of it is that a translator is forced to submit to the reality of something outside himself. And that reality, unlike a game of cards, is not circumscribed in advance. It has definite laws, but these are laws we can never fully master. Proust too called his novel a translation and not an invention, and he too recognised that the work of translation is a giving up of the Iago-self, the hard shell of habit and self-hood, a giving up which may perhaps lead to the discovery of that full self which he had glimpsed at times and for which he always yearned.

But this giving up is never easy. The search for form in Eliot, in Virginia Woolf, is often a desperate search. How desperate we see in the figure of Lily Briscoe, and in the life and death of Virginia Woolf herself. And even tougher artists, Stravinsky, Picasso, Wallace Stevens, will at moments give in to the temptations of a lordly narcissism. It is not easy to live abandoning the safety of the Iago-ego, accepting that it is only in a making which is a perpetual breaking of the ego that true fulfilment is possible.

13.   The struggle — the perpetual struggle — is very evident in the work of Beckett.

Beckett's work has always followed the pattern laid down at the end of his finest early story, 'Dante and the Lobster'. 'It's a quick death,' thinks Belaqua, watching the lobster go live into his aunt's boiling pot. For it had, we are told, 'about thirty seconds to live'. 'It is not', comes the reply, three words placed at the end of the story, impersonal, without quotation marks, the utterance of nature herself. We are not very far from Kafka's blood oozing between the great stones of the law.

Driven by the need to speak in order to utter the agony of the lobster, yet knowing that whatever he says will always only cover up that agony, render it acceptable instead of revealing it as the monstrosity it is, Beckett has moved slowly forward, shedding one skin after another in his effort to speak the truth. The Trilogy was of course the great testing ground for these matters, its very length an essential part of the process. First there was Molloy, still just about able to move; then Malone, dying in his closed room; finally the Unnamable, only able to identify himself in negative terms: not Molloy, not Malone, not Worm, only that which refuses to be named because each name, each history, will fix him, freeze him, deny him that which is most precious to him, his potential for movement, change. At the same time it is unbearable to live in a perpetual state of metamorphosis. The organism longs for stability, rest at last.

Non ego sed Democritus dixit, Sterne had copied out of Burton. In 'Not I' a mouth talks, seemingly unattached to any body. Between mouth and audience stands a shadowy figure. What is this figure? What is it doing there?

It has its instructions:

> Movement: this consists in simple sideways raising of arms from sides, and their falling back, in a gesture of helpless compassion. It lessens with each recurrence till scarcely perceptible at third. There is just enough pause to contain it as MOUTH recovers from vehement refusal to relinquish third person.

Why will the mouth not relinquish the third person? As always, there are two explanations for the same action. The mouth will not accept responsibility for what it says, denying that it is attached to any body. But it also knows that to speak in the first person is to perpetuate a falsehood, for that which is the source of utterance is always more than the ego. That is the drama. Somewhere something which is not the mouth keeps wanting it to accept to use the first person, but the only

acknowledgement of that unseen force is a violent denial; and
this is followed by the figure's gesture: '... and she found
herself in the — ... What?... who?... no!... she!... (*Pause
and movement*).' Once this is grasped we see that the compas-
sionate figure is deeply ambiguous: father confessor, but also
judge; friend, but also betrayer.

In *Company*, perhaps because it's a prose work and not a
play, the ambiguity is not resolved but tracked down. Again,
the narrator is unable to say 'I'. 'A voice comes to one in the
dark. Imagine.' The voice speaks, tells stories, but 'only a small
part of what is said can be verified.' All that can be ascertained
is that someone is lying on his back in the dark and a voice
comes to him, telling stories:

> Use of the second person marks the voice. That of the third
> that cankerous other. Could he speak to and of whom the
> voice speaks there would be a first. But he cannot. He shall
> not. You cannot. You shall not.

Of course it would be wonderful if he could: 'What an addition
to company that would be. A voice in the first person singular.
Murmuring now and then, Yes, I remember.' But though the
stories the voice tells are familiar, how is he to know if they are
stories about himself? It may simply be that the repetition has
made him imagine that they belong to himself. We say: This is
how I was; or, This is what I did — but in what sense is this 'I'
oneself? All that can be said is that to listen to the voice brings
him a sense of company, stops him being alone. All that can be
said with certainty is: 'Devised deviser devising it all for
company. In the same figment dark as his figments.' And so:

> Huddled thus you find yourself imagining you are not
> alone while knowing full well that nothing has occurred to
> make this possible. The process continues none the less
> lapped as it were in meaninglessness. You do not murmur
> in so many words, I know this doomed to fail and yet

persist. No. For the first personal and a fortiori plural pronoun had never any place in your vocabulary.

14.   And yet, curiously, out of the writer's renewed attempts to say 'I' and renewed refusal to come to rest in any position in which 'I' is less than his whole self, out of his perpetually repeated failure to find that fullness of voice for which James and Virginia Woolf longed, a certain voice does emerge. We say it is Eliot's, Muriel Spark's, Beckett's, though it does not belong to their social and public selves. This fullness of voice is something *we* register as we read, but it always eludes the writer himself. He who thinks he has it, loses it; he who goes on searching, releases it. The situation, as between writer and reader, will always be asymmetrical. For the writer it will always be the middle years, the time before, the time of failure, the time when it was necessary to start again. But for the reader the writer's middle years are truly that point whose centre is everywhere and whose circumference is nowhere, and in his work he sees the writer transform himself, as Mallarmé said death transforms us, into his total self: it always takes another to hear the voice, intuit the body.

15.   Since the argument of this lecture has been so dense and has ranged so widely, I would like to conclude by telling you a story.

The story concerns Dante, whose relevance to our theme has I hope been sufficiently demonstrated. I have mentioned his deep, absolutely primitive attachment to the *parlar materno*, the mother tongue. One might have thought that the fact of Dante's exile, his being forced to wander round the courts of Italy, finding shelter where it was offered, would have made it more likely that he would turn to the international language, Latin, when he came to write his epic. After all, two centuries later this was just what Erasmus did: he gave up being a native of Rotterdam and became a European citizen. Moreover, as I suggested, Dante was only too well aware of where love for the mother-tongue could lead: to the blind self-love of the giant Nimrod. Yet for Dante, as for Joyce, exile only strengthened the attachment to the speech of his childhood, and there was never really any doubt that when he came to write his life-work it would be in the vernacular. The poem itself, it would turn out, like Proust's novel, would both tell and show how he was able to do this and yet escape the Nimrod trap. And we will already find the general pattern of the entire poem in the overture, canto I of the *Inferno*, as we may find it in the overture to *A la recherche*.

Dante, you will remember, having come to in the dark wood, sees a mountain before him, with the sun shining over its summit. It is Spring, it is dawn, he is in the middle of his life. Everything says that this is a new beginning. He yearns for the light of the sun, and goes sprinting up the mountain. But at once he finds himself face to face with the three mysterious beasts, the third of which, the she-wolf

> put such heaviness upon me with the fear that came from sight of her that I lost hope of the height. And like one who is eager in winning but, when the time comes that makes him lose, weeps and is saddened in all his thoughts, such did that peaceless beast make me, as, coming on against me, she pushed me back, little by little, to where the sun is silent.

The images are significant here. Dante rushes up the mountain towards the source of light and salvation. But it takes only one obstacle to send him running down again just as fast. He has so little confidence in himself, so little awareness of what the journey really involves in terms of effort, of shedding the restricting layers of the self, that he is at once discouraged, 'like one who is eager in winning but, when the time comes that makes him lose, weeps and is saddened...'. He treats his action as a gamble which does not come off, a desperate throw of the dice. Ignoring the length and difficulty of the way, he tries to ignore as well the fact that it will inevitably involve him in time, in change, in a whole process which he cannot predict beforehand. He wants, somehow, to be already there. It is no surprise then that he falls back in despair, and that the wonderful synaesthetic image suggests that he falls back to a world not simply of darkness — the dark wood — but of a total, solipsistic silence: 'to where the sun is silent'.

The next lines make clear what is lacking:

> While I was ruining down to the depth there appeared before me one who seemed faint through long silence. When I saw him in that vast desert I cried to him: 'Have pity on me, whoever you are, shade or living man.'

The verbs 'ruining' and 'appeared' suggest a quite passive process. Dante does not see someone; he merely becomes aware of the fact that he is not alone. His response is instinctive and immediate:

> 'Miserere di me,' gridai a lui.
> (Have pity on me, I cried out to him.)

Miserere. A Latin word. Part of the liturgy. A small thing, but a momentous one. For in that moment Dante accepts his personal limits, accepts that he will need a guide, accepts the need *to speak*. And, accepting that, it is natural that he should speak in the language of prayer, the public language of the Church. Later he will ask Virgil to 'aiutami', to help him. Here he says: 'Pity me!'. *Miserere di me.*

The unknown 'other' is of course Virgil, though he introduces himself, rightly again, not as a great poet but as a Mantuan, born before Christ's time, and therefore debarred forever from salvation. This is as it should be. It is left to Dante to call him, in wonder, 'Oh my master and my author!' — 'lo mio maestro e il mio autore' — as it must always be the reader who responds to the writer in admiration. Dante begs Virgil, 'by that God whom you did not know', to guide him on his journey, and Virgil accepts. The first canto ends:

> Allor si mosse, e io li tenni dietro.
> (Then he moved, and I followed him.)

This word *mosse*, to move, is a key word in the *Commedia*. It is almost always associated with the word *amore*, love. Dante and Virgil can move, as can the souls in Purgatory; Nimrod is stuck forever, and even the romantic lovers, Paulo and Francesca, though they are not stuck in ice, are confined to their circle, and their motions are sheer reaction as they are hurled here and there by the erratic wind.

Now Dante *can* move, and so can eventually reach his goal, because he is prepared to trust another. Which means, in the end, because he is prepared to open his mouth and speak to another. Not to affirm himself, but to say: *miserere*. In the same way Dante the author, and we the readers, can move because we are prepared to trust language, recognising its limitations, but knowing that it is our surest path back to a lost fullness of the self. That ending to the first canto could be the epigraph to every artistic journey, the journey of the writer and that of the reader:

> Allor si mosse, e io li tenni dietro.

Only in the movement, venturing into the unknown, will Schoenberg's Moses find the word he lacks; only acknowledging the lack will make movement possible.

IV

'A Bird was in the Room'

———————→ •◦•◦• ←———————

1. So far in these lectures I have been talking about writing which is also art, literature. Today I want to examine the implications of some scribbled notes which have been preserved because their author was a great writer, but which it would, I believe, be a mistake to treat as being for that reason somehow special, explicable in terms of genius or even talent. On the contrary, I want to suggest that they take us as far as it is possible to go in understanding the relations of writing to the body at the simplest, most banal and literal level.

2. Let me read you a few of these scribbled notes. They are very brief:

> Aslant, that is more or less what I thought, so they can drink more; strip their leaves.

> A little water; these bits of pills stick in the mucus like splinters of glass.

> And move the lilacs into the sun.

> Do you have a moment? Then please lightly spray the peonies.

> A bird was in the room.

> Fear again and again.

> A lake doesn't flow into anything, you know.

By now we have come a long way from the day in the tavern garden when we

Put your hand on my forehead for a moment to give me courage.

These notes were written by Kafka. The circumstances in which he wrote them are explained by Max Brod in his note to the final pages of Kafka's *Letters to Friends, Family, and Editors*:

During his final illness at the sanatorium in Kierling Kafka was not supposed to speak [he had developed tuberculosis of the larynx], an injunction he obeyed most of the time. He communicated with Dora Dymant, Robert Klopstock, and others, by scribbling notes on slips of paper. Usually these notes were hints; his friends guessed the rest. A small selection has been published here from the originals in the possession of Dr. Klopstock...

3.   With this information in mind, let us look at the notes again. This time I will add a few more:

Aslant, that is more or less what I thought, so they can drink more; strip their leaves.

A little water; these bits of pills stick in the mucus like splinters of glass.

And move the lilacs into the sun.

Do you have a moment? Then please lightly spray the peonies.

A bird was in the room.

Mineral water — once for fun I could

Fear again and again.

A lake doesn't flow into anything, you know.

See the lilacs, fresher than morning.

By now we have come a long way from the day in the tavern garden when we

How wonderful that is, isn't it? The lilac — dying, it drinks, goes on swilling.

That cannot be, that a dying man drinks.

I was to have gone to the Baltic with her once (along with her girl friend), but was ashamed because of my thinness and other anxieties.

Put your hand on my forehead for a moment to give me courage.

So the help goes away again without helping.

How strange and resonant they are, these fragmentary messages coming at us out of the silence of the past. Why are they so moving — almost unbearably so? (I will quite understand if at this moment anyone wants to leave: to talk about them at all may strike one as an obscenity. Yet ultimately, I hope, my few comments will only serve to liberate them from commentary.) Clearly the situation has a great deal — everything perhaps — to do with it. After all, anyone could write down: 'A bird was in the room.' Would it have the same effect on us in another context?

The temptation is to say that since this is the case we are in danger of becoming grossly sentimental, and to leave the matter at that. But I think both notes and context have much to say to us, and that we should bear in mind Kafka's remark that man's chief sin is his impatience — and so approach the matter as carefully and patiently as possible.

4. It is possible, by reading the notes through enough times, to pick out certain recurrent themes and preoccupations.

Foremost among these is the pain Kafka is suffering in his throat, which makes it impossible for him to eat, and which makes even drinking an agony. Presumably it is because of this that he is obsessed by the flowers in his room and by their ability to drink even while dying, uprooted as they have been from the soil which is their natural habitat.

All his life of course Kafka's own disgust at himself and his body had made him peculiarly aware of others, especially animals, but even inanimate objects. He must be the only writer to have explored the suffering to which bridges are exposed, stretched out between two bits of land and liable, if trampled upon, to go crashing down into the foaming water beneath. The sympathy is utterly instinctive, and often borders on masochism, as in this passage from a letter to Felice:

> To be a large piece of wood, and to be pressed against her body by the cook, who with both hands draws the knife towards her along the side of this stiff log (approximately in the region of my hip) and with all her might slices off the shavings to light the fire.

In these last notes, however, there is a new quality of attention to things, and the relation of the flowers to himself and his plight is almost never made explicit.

In those last days Kafka was also correcting the proofs of his volume of stories, *A Hunger Artist*, and some of the notes refer to that. Robert Klopstock tells how

> when he had finished working on the proofs . . . tears rolled down his cheeks for a long time. This was the first and last time I ever saw any expression of emotion of this kind in Kafka. He has always shown superhuman self-control.

And, finally, there is a third strand running through the notes, made up of memories of the past which had clearly been welling up in Kafka as he lay cocooned in silence on the hospital bed: 'I was to have gone to the Baltic with her once (along with her girl friend), but was ashamed because of my thinness and other anxieties.'

But when we have accounted for all the slips of paper in this way, discovered what they all 'refer to', we have not gone any way towards explaining their effect. What I have just told you, in other words, will not have altered your initial response at all. Where then does the effect lie?

I think we can point to the immediate causes of their strange power, though it will take us a little more time to grasp the implications of these. In part it is the very fragmentariness of the notes that makes them so striking: 'Mineral water once for fun. I could — ' has a resonance that would be lacking were the sentence completed. But it is also a mysterious kind of redundancy — I can think of no other way of putting it — which contributes to the effect: 'A lake doesn't flow into anything, you know.' 'A bird was in the room.' The first is a platitude or tautology — I'm not enough of a grammarian to know just how one would describe it. The second is a plain statement of fact. Yet, written down, they seem to possess a strange resonance.

Why?

5. What a man says in his final moments has always been seen as possessing a particular authority. There is a persistent legend, made use of by more than one writer, that in those moments our whole life flashes before us, and though I suspect that the persistence of this legend is due to that human need for a real end which I discussed in the first lecture, it is certainly beyond question that a person's final pronouncements have a special significance. For in those moments a man passes beyond the normal reticences, hypocrisies and lies, and utters what he most firmly believes. In a rather obscure though suggestive passage Walter Benjamin even suggests that the authority of the traditional tale derives from its links with death:

It is, however, characteristic [he says] that not only a man's knowledge or wisdom, but above all his real life — and this is the stuff that stories are made of — first assumes transmissible form at the moment of his death. Just as a sequence of images is set in motion inside a man as his life comes to an end — unfolding the views of himself under which he has encountered himself without being aware of it — suddenly in his expressions and looks the unforgettable emerges and imparts to everything that concerned him that authority which even the poorest wretch in dying possesses for the living around him. This authority is at the very source of the story.

Whatever the truth of this may be, it is certainly a fact that the central story in Western culture derives *its* authority from its association with death. By his death Jesus — as he is at pains to point out beforehand — sets his seal not just on his own life but on the entirety of history. He signs the book of God, so to speak, and by so doing constitutes it as a meaningful whole.

Given the strength of this tradition it is not merely ironic, but profoundly shocking, that a man should be deprived of speech in those last moments. The matter becomes much more horrifying still when that man is Kafka. For if there is one thing that can be said without fear of contradiction about Kafka it is that he distrusted writing more than probably any literate person has ever done. Yet, in the end, Kafka is deprived of speech and condemned to writing.

To understand the full implications of this state of affairs for Kafka it is necessary to go back a little and trace in some detail the nature of his distrust of the written word.

6. Kafka, as we know, was never happier than when reading his stories aloud to his friends, and the one time he actually writes about himself with approval in his diary is after he has delivered a public speech on the Yiddish language at the time

of the visit of the East European Jewish actors to Prague. At the same time we know what doubts he had about writing. Like all of us he turned to writing — to the blank page and the pen — when he needed to try and make sense of his life, and like all of us he was frequently visited with the thought that writing, far from making sense of anything, only led to further entanglements and greater confusion. Only with Kafka both the sense of this and the ability to express it were a hundred times more powerful than they are for any of us.

Take the first paragraph of the letter he wrote to his father at the age of thirty-six, and which grew under his hand into a seventy-five page autobiography:

Dearest Father,

You asked me recently why I maintain I am afraid of you. As usual, I was unable to think of any answer to your question, partly for the very reason that I am afraid of you, and partly because an explanation of the grounds for this fear would mean going into far more details than I could even approximately keep in mind while talking. And if I now try to give you an answer in writing, it will still be very incomplete, because even in writing this fear and its consequences hamper me in relation to you, and because the magnitude of the subject goes far beyond the scope of my memory and power of reasoning.

Nevertheless, writing, in spite of everything, is the better alternative. In the quiet of his room, far from the insistent and frightening presence of the man to whom he wants, but fears, to speak, it will be possible for him to explore their relations and explain his position. Unfortunately, just this advantage is also a grave disadvantage. For writing, being of its nature a private activity, distorts the relationship even in the process of trying to explain it. The father's absence falsifies the whole operation right from the start, for his silence in the face of his son's unending stream of accusations is not the silence of aquiescence, but simply that of absence. It was no doubt Kafka's awareness of this which led him to give up the idea of ever sending the letter.

A similar paradox pervades his letters to the women with whom he was involved. There is no greater letter-writer than Kafka, and the letters here really were sent and received, but what were the letters *for*? He himself was well aware of the fact that the unending stream of letters to Felice and then to Milena were designed both to bind the women to him and to keep them at bay. In an extraordinary letter to Milena — but which of his letters is not extraordinary? — he writes:

> The great ease with which letters can be written must have brought into the world . . . a terrible dislocation of souls: it's a commerce with fantoms, not only with those of the recipient, but even with one's own; the fantom grows beneath the hand which writes, in the letter it is busy on, even more so in a series of letters where one corroborates the other and can call it to witness. Where did the idea spring from that letters would give men the means of communication? One can think of a person far away, one can hold a person who is near; the rest escapes human strength. Writing letters is presenting oneself naked before the fantoms; they avidly await the gesture. Written kisses do not reach their destination, the fantoms drink them on the way. Thanks to this nourishment they multiply at such an amazing rate . . . . The spirits will not die of hunger, but we will so die.

7.   Written kisses do not reach their destination, the fantoms drink them on the way. But these every-thirsty fantoms exist not only to create havoc with the letters we address to other people; they even intercept those we address to ourselves. If Kafka's letters to those he loved were destined both to hold on

to them and to keep them at bay, the same process can be seen at work, this time very much against his wishes, in the notes he wrote to himself, his diary jottings.

In 1917 the illness which had been hovering nearer and nearer finally caught up with him. He had a haemorrhage, wrote a letter informing Felice with just a hint of triumph that this had happened to him and he could now clearly no longer seriously consider himself a candidate for marriage, and took his first long spell of sick leave from the insurance company in which he had been working for virtually the whole of his adult life. Then he went to live for a while in the country with his favourite sister, Ottla. He had been there for scarcely a week when he wrote down in his diary:

> Have never understood how it is possible for almost everyone who writes to objectify his sufferings in the very midst of undergoing them; thus I, for example, in the midst of my unhappiness, in all likelihood with my head still smarting from unhappiness, sit down and write to someone: I am unhappy. Yes, I can even go beyond that and with as many flourishes as I have the talent for, all of which seem to have nothing to do with my unhappiness, ring simple, or contrapuntal, or a whole orchestration of changes on my theme. And it is not a lie, and it does not still my pain; it is simply a merciful surplus of strength at a moment when suffering has raked me to the bottom of my being and plainly exhausted all my strength. But then what kind of a surplus is it?

He is still pondering the mystery in 1921, for then he writes: 'Undeniably there is a certain joy in being able calmly to write down: "Suffocation is inconceivably horrible." Of course it is inconceivable — that is why I have written nothing down.'

As always with Kafka, what is given with one hand is taken away with the other. The first passage ends with a question to which there is no answer: 'But then what kind of a surplus is it?'

The second is a variant of the Cretan liar paradox which is so often the hidden form of Kafka's stories and remarks. For the phrase: 'that is why I have written nothing down' is of course itself written down. Does this mean that suffocation is then conceivable? No, for what is written down is that it is inconceivable. What is the nature of the joy one experiences in 'calmly' writing down such a sentence? What is the nature of the surplus strength which allows one to write: 'I am unhappy' in the midst of one's unhappiness? Like Derrida and his followers Kafka senses that as soon as we start to speak, to write, meaning is both made and unmade; that it escapes us even as we try to grasp it. But for him this is not a source of philosophical *interest*; it is a source of surprise and anguish.

For is writing down 'I am unhappy' in the midst of one's unhappiness a good or a bad thing? Is it a sign of imminent recovery or one more evasion, one more entanglement of the writer in his unhappiness? And from the point of view of the reader of these lines is it the genuine rendering of a painful truth or the cause of *his* entanglement in a further web of lies?

'Suffocation is inconceivably horrible.' Could a person who was really suffocating write that down? If Kafka were in fact suffocating it is doubtful whether he would have been able to write that line. But perhaps he is, after all, for only a person who *was* suffocating would realise that the experience was strictly speaking inconceivable. Besides, Kafka tells us that he has written nothing down.

A few months earlier he had jotted this in his diary:

> Anyone who cannot come to terms with his life while he is alive needs one hand to ward off a little his despair over his fate — he has little success in this — but with his other hand he can note down what he sees among the ruins, for he sees different (and more) things than do the others; after all, dead as he is in his own lifetime, he is the real survivor.

This assumes that he does not need both hands, or more hands than he has, in his struggle against despair.

We have often, in the last few years, encountered the moral ambiguity of the photographer-journalist taking a newsshot of innocent civilians being gunned down by an invading army. These tell the truth to the world and may actually play a part in ending the war in question, but how much of a truth is it when the photographer is excluded from the picture? Could he not have done something for the victims rather than simply photographing them? Perhaps the issue is not confined to journalism. It is impossible, in the above passage, to tell whether the person who wards off despair with one hand and scribbles with the other is worthier than the person who needs both hands to ward off despair. Looked at from one angle it seems that to manage to keep one hand free to write means that what will be written, because it will be written in the extremity of despair, will be truer, more honest, than other writing. The person who does so, Kafka tells us, sees more and more clearly than the others; he is not only the survivor, he is the survivor who lives to tell his tale. Yet one cannot help suspecting — as Kafka too seems to suspect — that there is something theatrical, false, in this one-handed warding off. Despair that only needs one hand to ward it off may not after all be real despair, and the writing produced by the other hand may therefore be even falser than most, since it will have pretended to be truer. (I do not need to remind you how often, in recent years, we have had writing foisted on us which has tried to claim our attention and approval by its assertion of painful honesty. Our unease with such writing stems from the fact that its very existence belies these claims, without the author's apparently being in the least conscious of this.)

8. By 1922 Kafka was no longer prepared to give writing the benefit of the doubt. In a terrible letter to Brod he writes:

Literature helps me to live, but wouldn't it be truer to say that it furthers this sort of life? Which of course doesn't imply that my life is any better when I don't write. On the contrary, then it is much worse, quite unbearable and with no other remedy than madness.... Creation is a splendid reward, but for what? Last night I saw very clearly... that these are wages earned in the devil's service.

Why? Because writing is vanity, pride. Ultimately, Kafka sees, writing only reinforces the essential feature of pride, our stubborn belief in our own immortality. Even at the moment of death, Kafka fears, even as he says to himself: 'This is the end', that *saying* will turn him away from the truth, will turn even death itself into another story.

Writing reinforces our belief in our own immortality by helping us to avoid the acceptance of our bodies. One of the little stories that make up Kafka's first published collection, *Meditation* (the very book he was putting together when he met Felice), shows that Kafka was already aware of the central issue in 1912. The story is called 'Bachelor's Ill-Luck' and it is short enough to quote in full:

It seems so dreadful to stay a bachelor, to become an old man struggling to keep one's dignity while begging for an invitation whenever one wants to spend an evening in company, to lie ill gazing for weeks into an empty room from the corner where one's bed is, always having to say good night at the front door, never to run up a stairway beside one's wife, to have only side-doors in one's room leading into other people's living-rooms, having to carry one's supper home in one's hand, having to admire other people's children and not even being allowed to go on saying: 'I have none myself', modelling oneself in appearance and behaviour on one or two bachelors remembered from one's youth.

111

That's how it will be, except that in reality, both to-day and later, one will stand there with a palpable body and a real head, a real forehead, that is, for smiting on with one's hand.

Even the real forehead, though, in this story as in all stories, is still only made of words, still only a product of the author's imagination. However much he says it is 'real', that 'real' is not real at all but only a word.

Kafka's strategy, over the next decade, consists in trying to force the reality of his body home upon his hero, as he would force it on himself and us. Take *Metamorphosis*. Everyone remembers the opening: 'As Gregor Samsa awoke one morning from uneasy dreams he found himself transformed into a gigantic insect.' And the story does not leave it at that. The paragraph continues:

> He was lying on his hard, as it were armour-plated, back and when he lifted his head a little he could see his dome-like brown belly divided into stiff arched segments on top of which the bedquilt could hardly keep in position and was about to slide off completely. His numerous legs, which were pitifully thin compared to the rest of his bulk, waved helplessly before his eyes.

Every movement Gregor tries to make drives his condition home to him. Yet the strange thing is how readily the human mind accommodates itself to circumstances. Not even death brings Gregor to a full realisation of who and what he now is. Indeed, the horror of the story lies in his — and our — inability ever to make sense of his transformed body.

Each new story of Kafka's is a fresh attempt to imagine what a real hand striking a real forehead would be like. It was perhaps in 1916, in what is no doubt his most repulsive story, that he came closest to it. You will remember that in 'In the Penal Colony' the camp commandant has devised a machine which slowly kills the guilty by cutting their indictment into their flesh. The commandant ran the colony with absolute authority, but he has been replaced by a more liberal person, and now his sole surviving disciple explains the workings of the machine to an explorer who is visiting the colony. It turns out that the condemned man does not know the sentence that has been passed on him. 'There would be no point in telling him. He'll learn it corporally, on his person,' explains the officer, who goes on to demonstrate exactly how the machine works. Basically, the idea is that little needles write the sentence all over the body of the condemned man:

> Of course the script can't be a simple one; it's not supposed to kill a man straight off, but only after an interval of, on an average, twelve hours; the turning point is reckoned to come at the sixth hour.... The first six hours the condemned man stays alive almost as before, he suffers only pain...

Then, at about that time, the man suddenly starts to understand:

> Englightenment comes to the most dull-witted. It begins round the eyes. From there it radiates.... You have seen how difficult it is to decipher the script with one's eyes; but our man deciphers it with his wounds. To be sure, that is a hard task: he needs six hours to accomplish it. By that time the Harrow has pierced him quite through and casts him into the grave, where he pitches down upon the blood and water and the cotton-wool. Then the judgement has been fulfilled, and we, the soldier and I, bury him.

Anyone who, like this man, believes that judgement can be fulfilled, will welcome his end as this one does. Grasping the fact that the entire administration of the colony is turning against him as the last sole representative of the old commander and his machine, he frees the culprit and himself settles into the machine, after having placed his indictment inside it: 'Be just'. The machine, however, perhaps with a mad logic of its own, having been started up again, proceeds to destroy itself and the officer along with it. The man dies as hideously as the previous victims, but this time with nothing at all having been written on his flesh: 'The Harrow was not writing, it was only jabbing, and the Bed was not turning the body over but only bringing it up quivering against the needles.' Before the explorer can do anything about it the whole hideous contraption has ground to a halt, with the dead man still stuck fast within it:

> And here, almost against his will, he had to look at the face of the corpse. It was as it had been in life; no sign was visible of the promised redemption; what the others had found in the machine the officer had not found; the lips were firmly pressed together, the eyes were open, with the same expression as in life, their look was calm and convinced, through the forehead went the point of the great iron spike.

This is the final manifestation of the Renaissance ideal we began with, that of a language which would be more than words, which would speak directly, be actively inscribed upon the body. But it is important to note that the hero or protagonist of the story is not the officer, but the explorer. And he is too detached or too clear-sighted ever to imagine that such an ideal fate might be possible. The story is Kafka's most terrible dramatisation of what might constitute a way out of the labyrinth of language in which he has for so long felt himself immured, unable to find any firm ground from which to launch himself into life, perpetually imbued with the sense that he has somehow not yet been born; but even as he writes it he seems to realise that it is still too Romantic in its self-destructiveness, and in his last stories the protagonist is even more peripheral to the action than the explorer. The mole in

his burrow, Josephine the mouse singer, the hunger artist —
they are more a source of impatience in others than anything
else. No one even bothers to condemn them to death, they
merely live and die on the edges of other people's consciousness,
and no sooner are they dead than they are forgotten:

> So perhaps we shall not miss her so very much after all,
> while Josephine, redeemed from the earthly sorrows which
> to her thinking lay in wait for all chosen spirits, will
> happily lose herself in the numberless throng of the heroes
> of our people, and soon, since we are no historians, will rise
> to the heights of redemption and be forgotten like all her
> brothers.

9. We are now perhaps a little nearer to understanding the
profound irony of Kafka's last illness. He who had always
mistrusted writing, he who had always longed for a writing
that would be more than mere words on paper, is now, in those
last moments, reduced to communicating only by means of
words on paper.

Yet we are not done with the ironies of this event. Kafka,
dying of this hideous illness in which it gradually became
impossible for him to eat and extremely painful for him to
drink, was still able to scribble. Yet one of the central themes
which run through his life and work is that of defining the
precise relations between food and words. To begin with, of
course, you cannot both speak and eat. Food nourishes you but
what do words do? The mouth mouthing words, the hand
forming words — are these not being turned from their true,
natural functions?

> I was, after all, depressed even by your mere physical
> presence [Kafka had written in the letter to his father]. I
> remember for instance how often we undressed together in
> the same bathing-hut. There was I, skinny, weakly, slight,

you strong, tall, broad. Even inside the hut I felt myself a
miserable specimen, and what's more not only in your eyes
but in the eyes of the whole world, for you were for me the
measure of all things.

But if the father's physical strength caused Kafka to be
disgusted with his own puny body, that very physicality was
also profoundly disgusting to him. The letter describes in
grotesque detail the father's way of cutting his nails at table,
his violent, unpredictable rages, his brutality with his family
and employees. Seen in this light he becomes a rapacious
carnivore, the creature who makes a success of his life by
ruthlessly shoving aside all who try to stand in his way.

No wonder Kafka starves himself, turns vegetarian, tries to
be even thinner than he is. As Canetti puts it in his moving little
book on Kafka: 'One must withdraw from violence, which is
unjust, by disappearing as much as possible. One makes
oneself very small or one transforms oneself into an insect.'
Kafka's most profound tendencies, he goes on, 'are to become
smaller and smaller, more and more silent, lighter and lighter,
till the final annihilation.'

Kafka's father was a self-made man. *His* father had been a
butcher in a village in Southern Bohemia. He had got to
Prague by dint of hard work and was determined to give his
family the advantages he had lacked. He had no time for intel-
lectuals or fooling around with words. But here was his son,
withdrawing from him and from what he had in mind for him,
and spending his time writing and reading. Yet what we have
here is no simple case of a sensitive youth revolting against
philistine parents. Kafka, in the letter, acknowledges that he
took to writing to escape his father, yet that in the end all his
writing was nothing else but a long-drawn-out — indeed, a
never-ending — leave-taking from him. And how could it be
anything else? How could he imagine he would ever be able to
get away from his father? For to get right away from him

would be to enter a world of total unreality, a world of childish make-believe. The very ease with which, through writing, it is possible to create alternative worlds, is enough to condemn writing as worse than useless, a total evasion.

At the same time, by one of the twists of the knife which Kafka seems so adept at discovering, the spirit of the father enters even the world of words. We find the following in an early diary entry:

> While dictating a rather long report to the district Chief of Police, towards the end, where a climax was intended, I got stuck and could do nothing but look at K., the typist, who, in her usual way, became especially lively, moved her chair about, coughed, tapped on the table and so called the attention of the whole room to my misfortune. The sought-for idea now has the additional value that it will make her be quiet, and the more valuable it becomes the more difficult it becomes to find it. Finally I have the word 'stigmatize' and the appropriate sentence, but still hold it all in my mouth with disgust and a sense of shame as though it were raw meat, cut out of me.

The word in his mouth is like a piece of raw meat, a portion of his own flesh. His instinctive vegetarianism, his almost anorexic behaviour later on in life, and his quite physical revulsion against words come together here in an eerie way.

Writing takes up space. To be a writer is to assert yourself at the expense of others. At the same time the words on the page are themselves assertive, elbowing others, with an equal right to be there, off the page. Kafka wants to curl up into a ball like a hedgehog, but in writing all he does is spread himself out until, like his father for the child Franz, he covers the entire world. The peculiar pathos of his last story, 'The Hunger Artist', lies in this. The crowd-dispelling fasting showman finally dies and is quickly cleared away to make place for the healthy and active panther, in whose jaws the spirit of freedom and health seem to lurk. But in the very writing of this story Kafka turns from fasting showman into carnivorous panther. And though this could be seen as the ultimate triumph of art, that would be to see it from the father's point of view. From Kafka's it is the ultimate failure of life, his life. And remember that it was the proofs of this that Kafka was correcting on his death-bed. Has there ever been such a tangling of truth and falsehood, such an interpenetration of motive?

10.   Kafka's father, I have said, was a self-made man, and he was determied that his children would not have to look back to the poverty and degradation he had known in his native village, but should absorb the dominant German culture and move ever forwards and up in the world. But for Kafka the whole thing seemed upside down. For him everything that is made only by the self is an imposition on the world, without meaning, and a sign of dehumanisation in that it implies the crushing of another human behing. The self-made man uses tradition for his own ends. Hence Kafka's horror at his father's purely social Judaism and his almost physical reaction to his father's use of a traditional expression when he found his son consorting with an unsavoury East European Jewish actor (who no doubt reminded him of a past he would rather forget): 'He who sleeps with dogs picks up fleas.' In the same way Iago had used proverbs for his own ends, while he busily worked upon the world to make it yield up the plot he needed from it.

But tradition is precisely that which is *not* questioned, that which is taken on trust. As Erich Heller has recently, and beautifully, put it:

> Every tradition, as long as it is intact, is a miniature paradise.... Not because tradition knows no suffering, far from it; but because it does not know the kind of curiosity that the serpent aroused in Eve.... For tradition is,

among a thousand other things, the silent and unconsciously wise agreement to curb one's curiosity...

But this is not quite right. As we saw when looking at *Othello*,
curiosity cannot be curbed; tradition exists when curiosity is
absent. Heller senses this, for he goes on to quote the end of
Kafka's little story, 'The Test':

> He asked me several things, but I couldn't answer, indeed
> I didnt't even understand his questions. So I said: Perhaps
> you are sorry now that you invited me, so I'd better go, and
> I was about to get up. But he stretched out his hand over
> the table and pressed me down. Stay, he said, that was
> only a test. He who does not answer the question has
> passed the test.

And Heller remarks: 'Perhaps it is the test of a tradition not
even to ask [questions].'

It would be wrong to imagine that Heller is talking about
anything abstract or esoteric. He is talking about what we
experience every day of our lives. For it is not the case that
there first is 'the tradition' and that then it vanishes. There are
countless traditions, as many perhaps as there are Wittgen-
steinian language-games. Thus to the person who has been
brought up celebrating Christmas as a family affair the sudden
decision to turn New Year's Day into a holiday will seem odd;
but to the person who has been brought up to think of the
family midwinter celebration as taking place on New Year's
Day, there is something incomprehensible and slightly comic
about the way people rush around getting worked up about
Christmas. Kafka's father had seen the degradation to which
immersion in a web of traditions can bring one; he was
determined to break out of this web, to forge a clean unclut-
tered future for himself and his children. In this he was of
course typical of many Jews of his time, as Kafka himself fully
realised. He also, like his generation of central European Jews,

perhaps had a good deal in common with those Englishmen of the seventeenth and eighteenth century of whom Iago was a kind of precursor and in whose midst the novel first emerged.

Kafka realised too that if all hope of salvation lay with such East European Jews as the actor Lowy and, indeed, the whole milieu from which his father was so keen to separate himself, he, Franz Kafka, could not partake of that salvation. In a letter to Milena he puts the matter quite clearly:

> We both know well many typical examples of Occidental Jews; of them all I am, as far as I know, the most typical; that is to say, exaggerating a little, that I don't have one second's peace, that nothing is given for me, that it is necessary for me to acquire everything, not only the present and the future, but also the past, that thing of which all men freely receive a portion; it too I must acquire, that is perhaps the hardest task...

This is the burden of all Kafka's work, and of all his actions. He would re-enter the tradition, or traditions, in which he might feel himself come alive, but such entry cannot start from him: he must be called in. And he knows that no one will call him. This is the drama of his love affairs and successive engagements. He wants to be married — but he cannot marry, because that demands a decision *from him*, and so abolishes precisely what he hopes to gain by marrying. The most one can do in this life, he tells his father, is to marry and raise a family and protect them against the world. But marriage, which would allow him to stand on the same footing as his father, and thus in one stroke set right the relations between them, would also turn him into the equivalent of his father, and that is one thing he instinctively will never do.

11.   Ultimately, he tells his father, marriage might prove to be his salvation, but what if it didn't? What if all it did was to make it impossible for him to write?

For writing, in spite of everything, is sensed instinctively as a good. And yet is that not to make writing the greatest betrayer of all? Writing mimes oneness with the tradition while all the time it is the product only of one man and his wilfulness. How can Kafka not view this with distrust, even with disgust?

12. It is time to return to the slips of paper Kafka scribbled on as he lay in the Kierling sanatorium, unable to speak. I want to suggest that why they are so moving is that, in the face of all I have said so far, of everything we have learnt about the place of writing in Kafka's life, and which should make of them only a bitter and ironic inversion of all our notions about the solemnity and authoritativeness of death — they are actually nothing of the sort. I began by pointing out how Kafka's being condemned to write down words on paper instead of speaking his last thoughts shows that we are never free of the labyrinthine ambiguities of writing, that there is no end to them. But it is also possible to say that what happens here is that, amazingly enough, writing itself is transformed into something supremely authoritative, and thus, when it is too late, allows Kafka to achieve what he had sought for all his life.

13. 'Mineral water once for fun. I could   '

The meaning, or the impact, comes from the fact that the message is broken off. What we understand is not the result of our *filling out* the sentence, completing it. It is the result of our feeling that the sentence could *never* be adequately filled out.

'A lake doesn't flow into anything, you know.'

Nothing here is being said that we didn't know. Why then do we feel that so much more is being said here than we ever knew before?

What these brief messages make manifest is this: human beings are always closed off to each other. What they convey in speech and writing is always both more and less than the words suggest. The well-made work is unsatisfactory precisely because it implies that meaning is complete, that nothing more needs to be said. But, as Kafka said to Janouch one day, there is always something left unaccounted for. The catch is that it must be left unaccounted for only after we have tried to account for everything. Otherwise it is merely unaccounted for by an oversight, because we have simply been impatient.

In these fragments that is no longer the case. 'A bird was in the room.' No one is allowed to say this, it is cheating, it is the cheapest trick of language. No one who feels a responsibility to language and to truth will simply write that down. If it is written and wasn't the case, then it is a lie. If it was the case, so what? No one, except Kafka, in this situation. He has earned the right, so to speak, to say what cannot otherwise be said. And when he writes that down what it conveys is not an element of fact, but a sensation of *wonder*. *That* Kafka should have chosen to record this, then, makes it something for us to wonder at. What it conveys is not meaning, not a message, but a person: Kafka. His longings, his ineluctable privacy, his inability to say what it is he wants to say.

Kafka's enforced silence is what speaks loudest to us. I suspect that it is also what we hear when we read any book that moves us. We listen to it as we don't to our friends. Proust was right to criticise Sainte-Beuve and Ruskin for refusing to distinguish art from conversation. In conversation we respond to the immediate. In art the immediate always has another dimension: we sense that it has been written. And written not by a computer or a penal settlement machine or in a universal language, but by a mortal man in a natural language.

Kafka had jotted down in his journal: 'My life a hesitation before birth.' And he had called Milena 'Mother Milena', half begging her to bring him to birth. Of course she could not do this. In a strange way, though, as we read him, we bring him to life within us. But we can only do this because as he writes he is about to die. And as we read we too are about to die, and so can experience what it is he experiences.

One of Kafka's most mysterious little stories concerns Odradek, that strange creature formed like one of those flat, star-shaped spools, with odd bits of wood sticking out of it at angles. 'He lurks by turns in the garrett, the stairway, the lobbies, the entrance hall.' When one asks him where he lives, he replies: 'No fixed address', and laughs. 'I ask myself, to no purpose, what is likely to happen to him? Can he possibly die? Anything that dies has had some kind of aim in life, some kind of activity, which has worn out; but that does not apply to Odradek.' Neither Czech nor German, neither man nor object, always on the move, unable to die, Odradek is the crystallisation of Kafka the imaginer of stories, one more example of the multitude of symbolic bodies he projects. But Kafka differs from Odradek by the simple fact, which we can experience but which, in a sense, Kafka can't, that he will die, that he is indeed now dead. It is because of this that Kafka's words come to us charged in a way those of Odradek could never be.

14.   But there is something else which is conveyed by those last notes. I find it difficult to be clear about it, but I think it is this: Kafka, who had always been so suspicious of writing, is, we have seen, forced in the end to rely upon it. And he is prepared to do so because he knows that someone will read what he has written: Dora Dymant, Robert Klopstock. What these fragments finally convey is the centrality of trust; they are an icon of trust.

To write down 'A bird was in the room' is to wish to share something with another person. It is not perhaps an important fact that is shared, but this is precisely why it demonstrates what it does. Kafka, who all his life had distrusted his own fluency, his own manipulative skill with words, who had felt as we have seen, that he was forever debarred from all traditions, forced to start everything from himself, through an effort of his own will — Kafka has here arrived at the point where there is either silence or the manifestation of trust. Because Klopstock is *there*, Kafka writes. It is as simple as that.

15. But here we come to the strangest thing of all. We see acted out before us, in slow motion and exaggerated form, so to speak, something which had always been the case, but which, without this, it might have been difficult to focus on. Kafka writes at this point, we have said, because of his trust in the friends who surround him. But why then, given all his doubts did he keep writing all his life?

Trust here takes on another dimension. It is trust simply in the ability of the hand to keep moving forward over the page. It is, finally, trust, against all the evidence, in the beneficial aspect of time, in movement as opposed to stasis.

I talked last week about the relation of trust to motion in Dante. Dante provided a beautiful illustration of this in the first canto of the *Commedia*. Kafka's life and death reveal it to us not as an idea or an insight, but as a simple fact.

You may remember that Kafka's ape, in his lecture to the Academy, told the august members of that assembly that he had never looked for freedom, only for a way out. He wanted simply to survive, and in circumstances a little less grim than he seemed to be condemned to. His way of doing so was to imitate the language of men. And so with Kafka. He too learned to imitate the language of men. But he often despaired of it. For language, it seemed, was utterly dependent on metaphor, on the girl who tends the fire, on the cat warming himself in front of the fire. Why reduplicate an already well-stocked world? Yet he went on needing a way out. And he found it by turning metaphor into metamorphosis.

Metaphor implies a fixed position from which we judge, choose and select. Metaphor leads to the compulsive imagining of the self as symbolic body: beetle, bridge, Odradek or mutilated corpse. And the end of such compulsive imagining is

autism, catalepsy, suicide. But if images belong to the dead
world of metaphor, the writing itself is metamorphosis, continuous transformation.

At basis all writing is the metamorphosis of the mechanical
movement of the hand into the infinite variety which constitutes letters, words, sentences. And just because Kafka's
refusal to accept *any* tradition on trust was so absolute, his final
acceptance of *this* is all the more moving. He may not have
trusted the world, or language, or literature, but his hand
moved unthinkingly over the paper, forming words. His moving hand was his Autolycus, no longer clearly labelled Fool or
disguised heroine, but a being possessed of the instinct for
survival and a trust in the bountifulness of time which nature
cannot let go unrewarded.

16.   We have reached rock bottom. Any movement we now
make will have to be sideways. And there are of course a
number of such movements which are open to us. We could
explore the contrast between the constant metamorphosis of
the moving hand in writing and the mechanical repetition of
masturbation, and go on to develop a set of contrasts between
an Oedipal organisation, genital sexuality and repressiveness
on the one hand, and freedom from such organisation, polymorphous perversity and perpetual foreplay on the other. I
think there is something in this kind of contrast, but that what
it tends to do is to polarise matters into good and bad where
instead I have tried to show the constant interplay of forces and
the perpetual contamination of the one by the other, and to
suggest that all gains are bought at a cost.

It would be possible, and perhaps more fruitful, to turn to
the kind of work being done by Luria and Sacks. Freud had
suggested that the language of hysteria corresponded only to
an imaginative image of the body and not to any physiological
reality. An arm, murderous only in fantasy, is punished by
paralysis, though physically there is nothing wrong with it.

Sacks has developed this insight in his studies of migraine and Parkinsonism. Here, he has shown, 'the symptoms are fixed and bounded by physiological connections', but 'they can constitute a bodily alphabet, or proto-language, which may subsequently be used as a symbolic language.' Here, then, and nowhere else, do we find the lived reality of that language of the Academy of Lagado which I discussed in my first lecture, a language that transcends words and speaks with reality itself. But the sufferer, of course, is more like the damned souls in Dante's *Inferno* than like Dante and Virgil. Though the distinction is a narrow one, and at times impossible to apply in practice, it is nonetheless a crucial one, for it is the distinction between the freedom to fulfil one's potential and the condemnation to an everlasting and compulsive repetition.

Yet the work of both Luria and Sacks suggests that the boundaries have constantly to be redrawn. In *The Man With the Shattered Skull* Luria examines the case of a young soldier who had part of his brain shot away in the war and spent the next twenty-five years laboriously trying to put together the pieces of his shattered world, to little avail. His extraordinary account of his attempts, beautifully edited and commented upon by Luria, show as does nothing else I know what a miracle human thought, memory and language are, though we take them so much for granted. Especially interesting is Luria's account of how Zasetsky was finally enabled to write when Luria persuaded him to stop worrying about the formation of individual letters, which was causing him terrible difficulty and anxiety, and instead to trust his pen, so to speak. 'Kinetic melody' is how Luria describes our normal habit of writing, and that beautiful phrase sums up a great deal of what I have been trying to say.

The work of Luria and Sacks also draws our attention to an important aspect of modern art. For, as I have suggested, the victims of disease and accident about whom they write, people who cannot remember anything, cannot forget anything, speak too fast or much too slowly — these alert us to what we take for granted most of the time: the incredible complexity of even the simplest mechanisms of speech, movement and writing. What we get from these accounts, though, is very much what we get from the best modern writing, and what we experience when we read Kafka's scribbled notes: 'A lake doesn't flow into anything you know.' 'A bird was in the room.' A sense of awe and wonder.

Few writers have been able to speak directly about these things. Wallace Stevens, in his last poems, those poems, as Randall Jarrell said, 'from the other side of existence, the poems of someone who sees things in steady accustomedness, as we do not; and who sees their accustomedness, and them, as about to perish' — Wallace Stevens is one of the few. Looking back, at over seventy, and asking himself what it had all been about, he gave a diversity of answers. One was the poem, 'The Planet on the Table':

> Ariel was glad he had written his poems.
> They were of a remembered time
> Or of something seen that he liked.
>
> Other makings of the sun
> Were waste and welter
> And the ripe shrub writhed.
>
> His self and the sun were one
> And his poems, although makings of the self,
> Were no less makings of the sun.
>
> It was not important that they survive.
> What mattered was that they should bear
> Some lineament or character,
>
> Some affluence, if only half-perceived,
> In the poverty of their words,
> Of the planet of which they were a part.

In the old days, at the time of 'The Man With the Blue Guitar', Stevens had worried about whether it is up to the poet to make the world, to discover its true shape, or whether such making is a distortion. In a sense he has passed beyond such questions now. The planet is on the table, for it is only conjured up in his poem. It is there, like a child's globe perhaps, to be turned this way and that. But the 'it' which we turn about, the poem there before us, is also an acknowledgement that it is only a part of the world, one more element within it. And yet not a 'mere' part, but a part in the sense of 'playing a part'. 'That's it'. Stevens had understood as he was finishing 'Auroras of Autumn', 'The lover writes, the believer hears, The poet mumbles, the painter sees, Each one, his fated eccentricity, As a part, but tenacious particle, Of the Skeleton of the ether, the total...'.

The poet mumbles, but this is not a wholly private activity. In 'To an Old Philosopher in Rome' Stevens apostrophises Santayana, urging him

> Be orator but with an accurate tongue
> And without eloquence, O half-asleep,
> Of the pity that is the memorial of this room
>
> So that we feel, in this illumined large,
> The veritable small, so that each of us
> Beholds himself in you, and hears his voice
> In yours, master and comiserable man.

As we read these lines we are the old philosopher in Rome, and we are Stevens as he imaginatively enters the old man's world. But we are also, strangely, more ourselves than we were before. Each of us hears his voice in Stevens's, and this means that we hear ourselves saying what we did not know we could say, in a tone we didn't know was ours, but which, hearing, we recognise as the actualising of what had always been latent. The same thing happens, I would suggest, when we read, at the end

of the volume of Kafka's letters: 'A bird was in the room.'
Saying it, we are Kafka in that room, in that loneliness. And so
that loneliness is something shared.

17.   In conclusion, I would like to make two points. The first
has to do with the notion of trust which has figured so
prominently in these lectures. It seems to me to be a concept
which it is easier for a Jew than for a Christian, especially a
Protestant, to understand. Ignaz Maybaum, in a fine lecture
on the binding of Isaac, made the point that for the Jew the
story is, at a profound level, never in doubt. He trusts God as
Isaac trusts his father; as Isaac says 'Here am I' when his father
calls him, so Abraham says 'Here am I' when God calls him.
But for Kierkegaard, as for Paul before him, all is a matter of
crisis, faith, a faith beyond the bounds of reason.

   This is very suggestive. I bring it in not to claim Kafka for
Judaism, which would be nonsense. I hope I have shown that
trust is ultimately something instinctively human, lying somewhere in the region between brain and wrist, and that it has
nothing to do with ethnic or religious affiliations. But if I have
been right in the general historical trend of my argument, if
there was indeed a shift of consciousness in the sixteenth and
seventeenth centuries, and if Iago and Malvolio are typical of
the new spirit which will take nothing on trust, then it may be
helpful to bring to the fore this opposition between trust and
faith. Perhaps by stressing the Jewishness of the concept of
trust I am only trying to highlight its opposite, which for
convenience we can call the Protestant spirit, and which seems
to infect all thinking men in the course of the years 1500 to
1700.

   I am, in a sense, only repeating what Nietzsche argued, and
what recent thinkers like Dan Sperber have suggested, that the
will to truth, to interpretation, is not a given, but is an aspect of
our culture, a culture forged in the sixteenth and seventeenth
centuries. 'The attribution of sense is an essential aspect of

symbolic development in our culture' is how Sperber puts it. The difficulty with such notions is that the very vocabulary with which we deal with these matters is itself derived from this culture. Our problem is to get behind that and to discover why it came about and what aspects of life it hides or distorts.

And it is here that I come to my second point. Imaginative literature can help us with our task as nothing else can. My exploration of *Tristram Shandy* and *Othello* will, I hope, have made that plain. It will also have been evident to you that in the course of these lectures I have not hesitated to make use of Freud, or to borrow from anthropologists and philosophers when it suited me. Purists may feel that I have been employing the vocabulary or concepts of other disciplines in too loose and unsystematic a fashion. I make no apology. Literary criticism has for too long, it seems to me, been overimpressed by what it sees as other, 'harder', more 'relevant' disciplines. It has felt that it cannot understand the works of the imagination unless it first masters the thought and vocabulary of linguistics or psychoanalysis. But is this not just one more example of the lack of trust, of the Iago-ego at work? George Craig, in the essay on Proust to which I referred in my first lecture, made a very important point when he began a sentence with the words: 'We can, with Freud and Lacan — and a little imagination...'. Nothing I have been talking about has to do with any kind of specialised discipline: a little imagination, a little attention, that is all that is required. Naturally, if there are imaginative and brilliant men working in other fields, it would be folly to ignore them. But if I am correct in what I have been saying, it may be that the taking of so much on trust, the perpetual lack of certainty which is the hallmark of the imagination, may be *truer to the facts* than the certainties of scientists and philosophers.

18. In keeping with this credo, let me end not with a statement or a summary, but with a brief commentary on

one of the endings of a writer who knew all about endings.

The most moving moment in Shakespeare is not the death of Hamlet or Othello. It is not even the death of Lear. It is the moment when Lear talks to himself over the dead body of Cordelia. It is so moving because it is seen only in profile, as it were. It is not something we hear but, like Kafka's last notes, something we overhear. Nothing that Lear says at this point advances the plot, nothing is, in a sense, necessary. What Lear says is simple too, far from the great poetry of so much of the play; and, besides, he is fooling himself. But it is just because the language is inadequate to the situation, just because we sense in Lear's blindness a dramatisation of our own perpetual and incorrigible blindness, that we are so deeply moved. Though Shakespeare is wonderfully tactful with his ending, Edgar's last words in particular can only strike us as too full and confident for what has gone before. They face us directly, so to speak, guiding our responses, filling in the gaps for us, denying the emptiness we have just glimpsed, which may after all be the space we really need if we are to become fully alive.

Shakespeare never quite found a way of making full use of what the happy accident of the plotting of *Lear* had given him. But something of that feeling is conjured up again, though seemingly in very different guise, at the very end of his last play. Prospero comes forward and addresses the audience:

> Now my charms are all o'erthrown,
> And what strength I have's mine own,
> Which is most faint: 'tis true,
> I must be here confined by you,
> Or sent to Naples. Let me not,
> Since I have my dukedom got,
> And pardoned the deceiver, dwell
> In this bare island by your spell:
> But release me from my bands
> With the help of your good hands:

131

Gentle breath of yours my sails
Must fill, or else my project fails,
Which was to please. Now I want
Spirits to enforce, Art to enchant;
And my ending is despair,
Unless I be relieved by prayer,
Which pierces so, that it assaults
Mercy itself, and frees all faults.
    As you from crimes would pardoned be,
    Let your indulgence set me free.

We know this so well that it is perhaps difficult to see it for what it is. We all know how Victorian critics read it as Shakespeare's farewell, not Prospero's, and such critics have come in for a lot of stick in the past fifty years. I have no wish to take their side. Yet certain conclusions seem inescapable.

Prospero is speaking. Many references in the passage link it firmly to the play we have just seen. On the other hand it is a new Prospero, not the one we have had before us so far. What strength he has is now his own. He has buried his magic book and is now an ordinary mortal. At this point he makes an odd appeal to the audience: 'Let me not, Since I have my dukedom got, And pardon'd the deceiver, dwell In this bare island by your spell...' It is now we, the audience, who wield the magic power, and Prospero who is at our mercy as Caliban was at his. Imperceptibly, too, we have been moving out of the fiction. Now it is the actor who says: So far I have been speaking someone else's lines, now I speak to you in my own words, and I need your help — though of course he accepts that the help we give him is conditional on his having entertained us earlier.

And now, imperceptibly again, we move into yet another context. 'Release me from my bands With the help of your good hands' is straightforward enough. 'Gentle breath of yours my sails Must fill, or else my project fails' is just about conceivable as a call to the audience to cheer as well as clap. But 'my ending is despair,   Unless I be relieved by prayer' is something new. We could say that Shakespeare is here emerging from the figure of the actor who has himself emerged from the figure of Prospero. But the lines haunt us just because *he cannot quite emerge.* Just as the actor, having dropped his Prospero voice or removed his Prospero cloak, can never quite dispel the awareness that even these lines have been written for him, are not 'really' his; so whoever or whatever is behind Prospero, even though he substitutes simple octosyllabics for the more usual pentameter, can never quite speak *in propria persona.* The gap remains. It is the necessary fiction, for 'even the absence of imagination had itself to be imagined', as Stevens said. And just as Stevens ends one of his great last poems with the injunction: 'call it, again and again,   The river that flows nowhere, like a sea'; so here Shakespeare ends with an injunction: 'As you from crimes would pardoned be,   Let your indulgence set me free.'

And so we clap and the actors take their bows. But their freedom is ambiguous, both desired and dreaded, a release from the constraints of the role, but a release into what? Tomorrow they will return to the liberating prisons of those roles.

Shakespeare lives in Prospero, yet he also dies a little behind the mask. The actor too both lives and dies. He discovers possibilities within himself as he speaks the lines of another, and it is we, the audience, who help him do this: because *we* are there, *he* is. And we too, watching, then applauding, undergo a similar process, moving perpetually between constraint and freedom, and between a constraint that releases and a freedom that imprisons.

19.   Shakespeare is, in the end, ready to accept the constraints. The epilogue is, after all, an accepted part of any play. Shakespeare may almost break its mould, but he will never

break it completely; he is too conscious of the benefits of remaining within it. Modern writers, equally conscious perhaps, have nevertheless felt it necessary to break and to go on breaking all the moulds. And yet, as Kafka said, there is always something left unaccounted for. I too have attempted to get as close as possible to a certain truth which it seemed important to try and articulate, but I have had, ultimately, to content myself with what may well be seen as a series of tallish stories. In the end I have to trust you to make up for yourselves what can never be said.

Notes

p. 3. *Borges recounts.* 'The Garden of Forking Paths', in *Labyrinths*, eds. D. A. Yates and J. E. Irby, Harmondsworth, 1970.

p. 4. *Swift's description. Gulliver's Travels*, Book III, Ch. V. The passage is so interesting it is worth quoting in full:

> The other, was a scheme for entirely abolishing all words whatsoever: And this was urged as a great advantage in point of health as well as brevity. For, it is plain, that every word we speak is in some degree of diminution of our lungs by corrosion; and consequently contributes to the shortening of our lives. An expedient was therefore offered, that since words are only names for *things*, it would be more convenient for all men to carry about them, such *things* as were necessary to express the particular business they are to discourse on. And this invention would certainly have taken place, to the great ease as well as health of the subject, if the women in conjunction with the vulgar and illiterate had not threatened to raise a rebellion, unless they might be allowed the liberty to speak their tongues.... However, many of the most learned and wise adhere to the new scheme of expressing themselves by *things*; which hath only this inconvenience attending it; that if a man's business be very great, and of various kinds, he must be obliged in proportion to carry a greater bundle of *things* upon his back, unless he can afford one or two strong servants to

attend him. I have often beheld two of those sages almost sinking under the weight of their packs, like pedlars among us; who, when they met in the streets would lay down their loads, open their sacks, and hold conversation for an hour together; then put up their implements, help each other to resume their burthens, and take their leave.

p. 4. *Stravinsky, in an interview.* Reprinted in *Dialogues and a Diary*, London, 1968. See also Calvino's *Note* to his *The Castle of Crossed Destinies*, tr. William Weaver, London, 1977.

p. 9. *Lévi-Strauss.* Quoted in John Mepham, 'The Structuralist Sciences and Philosophy', in *Structuralism*, ed. D. Robey, London, 1972.

p. 11. *As I suggested.* In *The World and the Book*, London, 1971, especially Ch. 4, 'Rabelais: Language and Laughter'. Terence Cave, *The Cornucopian Text*, Oxford, 1979.

p. 19. *Eighteenth-century printers.* See the fascinating essay by Roger Moss, 'Sterne's Punctuation', forthcoming in *Eighteenth-Century Studies*. It overlaps with my own discussion of Sterne in more than one place.

p. 21. *George Craig.* 'The "Petite Phrase" and the sentence', forthcoming in *Journal of the History of European Ideas*.

p. 23. *Walter Benjamin.* In the first draft of 'What is Epic Theatre?', in *Understanding Brecht*, tr. Anna Bostock, London, 1975.

p. 23. *'Theses on the Philosophy of History'.* In *Illuminations*, tr. Harry Zohn, London, 1970.

p. 25. *Traditional story-telling.* A splendid description of a *ceilidh* or Highland story-telling session, is quoted from Alexander Carmichael's *Carmina Gadelica* in the introduction to Katharine Briggs's *British Folk Tales and Legends: A Sampler*, London, 1977:

> The house of the story-teller is already full, and it is difficult to get inside and away from the cold wind and sleet without. But with that politeness native to the people, the stranger is pressed to come forward and occupy the seat vacated for him beside the houseman. The house is roomy and clean, if homely, with its bright peat fire in the middle of the floor. There are many present — men and women, boys and girls. All the women are seated, and most of the men. Girls are crouched between the knees of fathers or brothers or friends, while boys are perched wherever — boy-like — they can climb.... The houseman is twisting twigs of heather into ropes to hold down thatch, a neighbour crofter is twining quicken roots into cords to tie cows, while another is plaiting bent grass into baskets to hold meal. The housewife is spinning, a daughter is carding, another daughter is teasing, while a third daughter, supposed to be working, is away in the background conversing in low whispers with the son of a neighbouring crofter. Neighbour wives or neighbour daughters are knitting, sewing or embroidering. The conversation is general.

Other vivid examples of the atmosphere of oral story-telling are to be found in David Thomson's marvellous *The People of the Sea*, London, 1965. I suspect that most of the critical and philosophical problems that arise in the study of works of literature stem from the fact that when we read a book we can do nothing else, while when we listen to a story being told our hands can be active. The apparently only partial attention accorded the story-teller in the above quotation may perhaps be a better way of taking in stories than the full attention educational institutions tend to try to foster.

p. 26. *The Puritan sense that it is wrong to listen to stories.* See the interesting essay by J. Paul Hunter, 'The Loneliness of the Long-Distance Reader', *Genre*, vol. X, No. 4, from which the following examples are taken.

p. 34. *'Everything and Nothing'* In *Labyrinths*. I have preferred the translation by Mildred Boyer in *Dreamtigers*, London, 1973.

p. 36. *Kermode*. In *Encounter*, November 1964.

p. 36. *A Natural Perspective*. New York, 1965.

p. 41. *Terence Cave*. 'Recognition and the Reader' in *Comparative Criticism, A Yearbook*, ed. E. Shaffer, Cambridge, 1980.

p. 44. *Virginia Woolf. The Diary of Virginia Woolf. Volume III: 1925-1930*, London, 1980, pp. 300-301. It is interesting that an earlier entry in the same volume (p. 182) registers a resistance to Shakespeare's verbalism, and with specific reference to *Othello*:

> I was reading Othello last night, and was impressed by the volley and volume and tumble of his words: too many I should say, were I reviewing for the Times. He put them in when tension was slack. In the great scenes, everything fits like a glove. The mind tumbles and splashes among words when it is not being urged on: I mean, the mind of a very great master of words who is writing with one hand. He abounds. The lesser writers stint.

p. 46. *A. D. Nuttall. William Shakespeare: The Winter's Tale*, London, 1966.

p. 49. *John Bayley. The Characters of Love*, London, 1960, Ch. 3.

p. 50. *But Iago's is a private, anti-social nature. Twelfth Night* once again provides us with a version of this, in the comic mode: Malvolio appearing before Olivia in festive dress, smiling 'his face into more lines than is in the new map with the augmentation of the Indies' (III, ii, 91-3). Like Iago, Malvolio is only *imitating* jollity, but he is ridiculous rather than threatening because he is not the deceiver but the deceived.

p. 51. *may not themselves know 'what is going on'.* Compare Nuttall's comments on Act I of *The Winter's Tale*, op.cit.

p. 53. *despairing Swiftian way.* See *A Tale of a Tub*, the 'Digression on Madness'.

p. 55. *Preface to Plato.* Oxford, 1963.

p. 64. *Henry James in his Notebooks. The Notebooks of Henry James*, eds. F. C. Matthiessen and K. B. Murdock, New York, 1961, p. 106. Similar outbursts punctuate the pages of the *Notebooks*.

p. 69. *A recent historian.* Jaques Le Goff, *La civilisation de L'Occident mediéval*, Paris, 1972, p. 342.

p. 70. *Dragonetti.* 'Dante face a Nemrod', *Critique*, August-September 1979, p. 691. The whole issue is devoted to 'Le mythe de la langue universelle' and contains many interesting articles apart from Dragonetti's.

p. 74. *Eliot.* Quoted in Hugh Kenner, *The Invisible Poet*, London, 1960.

p. 77. *Pierre Menard.* 'Pierre Menard, Author of the Quixote', in *Labyrinths*.

p. 79. *cutting a quotation out of its place in a continuum.* Antoine Compagnon's *La seconde main*, Paris, 1979 unfortunately came to my notice after these lectures were written. It is a detailed study of 'le travail de la citation' and touches on many of the themes dealt with in this lecture.

p. 80. *to remove the obstacles.* For a discussion of this in relation to *Ulysses*, see Roger Moss, 'Difficult language' in *The Modern English Novel*, ed. G. Josipovici, London, 1976.

p. 86. *Alexander Goehr.* 'Some thoughts about Stravinsky', in the programme for the Stravinsky Festival, Part II, Royal Festival Hall, January-February 1981.

p. 86. *Years later he was to say. Expositions and Developments*, London, 1962, pp. 122, 115.

p. 87. *Daix and Rosselot. Picasso: The Cubist Years, 1907-1916*, London, 1980.

p. 90. *The epic poet.* See especially, in the wake of Parry and Lord, G. Nagler, *Spontaneity and Tradition*, Berkeley 1974, and B. Peabody, *The Winged Word*, Albany, 1975.

p. 90. *Once upon a time.* For a fuller discussion of what follows see my 'Text and Voice', in *Comparative Criticism, A Yearbook*, ed. E. Shaffer, Cambridge, 1980.

p. 96. *the middle years.* The reference is of course to James's great short story, especially to its marvellous closing pages.

p. 99. *mosse.* The third word in the cluster is *tornare*. Those in Purgatory have shown, in life, a suppleness, an ability to change, to move, to turn, which is not to be found among the rigid souls in Hell.

p. 101. *Max Brod.* The note is on p. 493 of the English edition. The 'Conversation Slips' occupy pages 416-23.

p. 104. *Walter Benjamin.* 'The Storyteller', in *Illuminations.*

p. 105. *He signs the book of God.* See my essay, 'Dialogue and Distance' in *Ways of Reading the Bible*, ed. M. Wadsworth, Brighton 1981.

p. 115. *Food and words.* There are some suggestive remarks on this topic in G. Deleuze and F. Guattari, *Kafka, pour une littérature mineure*, Paris, 1975.

p. 116. *Canetti.* Kafka's Other Trial, tr. C. Middleton, London, 1974. This now forms the Preface to the Penguin edition of the *Letters to Felice.*

p. 118. *Erich Heller.* 'Investigations of a Dog and Other Matters', in *The World of Franz Kafka*, ed. J. L. Stern, London, 1980.

p. 124. *Metaphor.* For a different view of metaphor — closer, in fact, to my concept of metamorphosis, see Bernard Harrison's 'Metaphor and Interpretation'. My own argument depends on a much more naive and physical notion of metaphor and metamorphosis than philosophers would probably be willing to accept.

p. 125. *cost.* I am thinking in particular of the work of Norman Brawn and Deleuze and Guattari. Jakobson, who is one of the few linguists never to have shied away from considering language in relation to the body, has also been very clear about the cost to the child of acquiring speech. In *Child Language, Aphasia and Phonological Universals*, for example, he argues that the babble of the child contains all sounds but that most of these are lost with the first acquisition of speech. He goes on:

In place of the phonetic abundance of babbling, the phonemic poverty of the first linguistic stages appears, a kind of deflation which transforms the so-called 'wild-sounds' of the babbling period into entities of linguistic value.

He proceeds to show that a full grasp of language, both active and passive, depends on articulation and so on the ability to differentiate. The crucial moment is when the child moves from the undifferentiated cry (*aaaa*) which is pure emotional expression, to the call (*mama*), which is his entry into the world of language, culture and symbolism. What this suggests is that a loss of self, a sacrifice of the immediate and the physical is required in the interests of long-term gains. But ambiguities abound. One remembers how Freud came to see repetition itself as a manifestation of the death wish; yet the denial of the physical involved in articulation can itself lead to the permanent installation of the super-ego and thus of the death-wish in another form.

p. 125. Luria and Sacks. Luria died in 1977. In his fascinating article, 'Witty Ticcy Ray', in the *London Review of Books*, Vol. 3, No. 4, March 1981, Sacks talks a little about the relation of the two men. The quotations from Sacks come from the revised edition of *Migraine*, London, 1981.

p. 129. *Ignaz Maybaum. The Sacrifice of Isaac*, London, 1959.

p. 129. *Jewishness of the concept of trust.* See my essay, 'Dialogue and Distance' in *Ways of Reading the Bible*, and 'The Irreducible Word' in the special issue of *European Judaism* on the Bible, ed. Jonathan Magonet, Autumn 1981.

p. 129. Sperber. *Rethinking Symbolism*, Cambridge, 1975.

Acknowledgements

A version of Chapter IV first appeared in the June 1981 issue of *Quarto*. I am grateful to the editor for permission to reprint.